I0757033

KATE HALE

Encouraging Emotional Intelligence

Helping Children Recognize and Manage Feelings

Copyright © 2024 by KATE HALE

All rights reserved. No part of this publication may be reproduced, stored or transmitted in any form or by any means, electronic, mechanical, photocopying, recording, scanning, or otherwise without written permission from the publisher. It is illegal to copy this book, post it to a website, or distribute it by any other means without permission.

First edition

This book was professionally typeset on Reedsy.
Find out more at reedsy.com

Contents

Introduction 1

What is Emotional Intelligence? 8

Emotional Development in Children 18

The Science Behind Emotional Intelligence 28

Helping Children Identify Their Emotions 38

Understanding and Validating a Child's Emotions 49

Teaching Empathy Early On 57

Teaching Self-Regulation to Children 69

Problem-Solving Skills for Emotional Situations 79

Mindfulness and Emotional Control 89

Developing Healthy Relationships with Emotional Intelligence ... 100

Managing Peer Pressure and Bullying 109

Modeling Emotional Intelligence at Home 118

Emotional Intelligence in the Classroom 127

Digital Age Challenges: Managing Screen Time and Emotions ... 138

Fostering Resilience in Children 147

Emotional Intelligence and Academic Success 156

Preparing Children for Future Challenges 165

Conclusion 174

Introduction

Why Emotional Intelligence Matters

Emotional intelligence (EI), often referred to as emotional quotient (EQ), is a crucial skill set that shapes a child's ability to understand and manage their emotions, interact positively with others, and navigate life's challenges effectively. While traditional measures of intelligence, such as IQ, have long been considered essential predictors of success, research increasingly shows that emotional intelligence plays an equally, if not more, important role in personal and social success. Emotional intelligence impacts every facet of a child's development—from forming friendships to academic performance and even their future mental health.

One of the core reasons emotional intelligence matters is its direct impact on relationships. Children with high emotional intelligence can recognize their own feelings and the emotions of others, which fosters empathy, cooperation, and strong interpersonal connections. For instance, a child who can recognize when a peer is feeling sad or left out is more likely to offer comfort or include that child in a game. This empathetic behavior creates a nurturing environment that benefits not only the emotionally intelligent child but also their social group. Over time, this skill helps build the foundation for meaningful, lasting relationships, a critical component for success and well-being later in life.

Moreover, emotional intelligence is essential for mental health. Children who can identify and express their emotions are less likely to internalize negative feelings, which reduces the risk of anxiety, depression, and behavioral issues. When children learn to manage frustration, fear, or sadness early on, they develop resilience. This resilience enables them to cope with stress in healthy ways, helping them bounce back from failures or setbacks, such as a poor grade on a test or a disagreement with a friend. In contrast, children who lack emotional awareness might struggle with these experiences, potentially leading to feelings of inadequacy or hopelessness.

Another critical reason emotional intelligence matters is its influence on academic success. Emotionally intelligent children tend to be better learners because they can manage their emotions, focus on tasks, and persevere through challenges. They are also more adept at working in teams, a skill that is increasingly valued in educational settings. For example, group projects often require students to collaborate, listen to differing opinions, and regulate their frustrations—skills that are closely tied to emotional intelligence. Additionally, emotionally intelligent students are more likely to have positive relationships with teachers and classmates, creating a supportive learning environment that enhances academic engagement and achievement.

The role of emotional intelligence extends into problem-solving and critical thinking as well. Children who understand their emotions can navigate complex social situations with more clarity and confidence. For example, when a child is upset or angry, emotional intelligence allows them to step back, evaluate the situation, and respond in a way that is constructive rather than reactive. This ability to pause, reflect, and act thoughtfully is invaluable as children grow older and face more complicated challenges in school and social interactions.

Emotional intelligence also supports physical well-being. Emotionally intelligent children are less likely to engage in risky behaviors, such as substance abuse or delinquency, as they grow older. They are more aware of the long-term consequences of their actions and can regulate impulsive behaviors that could harm their health. This self-regulation, paired with a deeper understanding of their own needs and boundaries, helps children make healthier decisions about their bodies, their relationships, and their environments.

In conclusion, emotional intelligence matters because it is integral to a child's overall development. It influences their ability to form relationships, succeed academically, maintain mental health, and make positive decisions. Cultivating emotional intelligence from a young age sets children up for a lifetime of success and well-being, making it one of the most valuable skills parents, teachers, and caregivers can nurture.

The Role of Parents, Teachers, and Caregivers

Parents, teachers, and caregivers play a fundamental role in fostering emotional intelligence in children. These individuals are often a child's first point of contact with the world, shaping their emotional development through daily interactions, guidance, and modeling. Children learn about emotions by observing and interacting with the adults around them, making the role of parents and educators particularly crucial in developing a child's emotional intelligence.

Parents are a child's first teachers in emotional intelligence. From infancy, children look to their parents for cues on how to respond to the world. The way parents react to their child's emotions, whether it's through soothing, acknowledging, or dismissing feelings, has a profound impact on how the child understands and processes their own emotions. For instance, when a parent calmly acknowledges a child's frustration over a toy that won't work and offers support, the child learns that it's okay to feel frustrated and that there are constructive ways to deal with such emotions. In contrast, if a parent dismisses or criticizes the child's feelings, the child may internalize the belief that their emotions are invalid or unacceptable.

Furthermore, parents who model emotional intelligence by expressing their own emotions in healthy ways provide a powerful example for their children. When parents show empathy, regulate their anger, or openly discuss their feelings, children learn that emotions are a normal and manageable part of life. This modeling is especially important in stressful situations, such as disagreements or disappointments. For example, a parent who remains calm during a heated conversation demonstrates to the child that it's possible to manage emotions constructively, even in challenging moments. Over time, children internalize these behaviors and apply them in their own emotional experiences.

Teachers also have a significant influence on emotional intelligence, particularly in the structured environment of the classroom. School is often the first place where children are expected to navigate complex social situations independently, making it an ideal setting for teaching emotional intelligence. Teachers can foster emotional intelligence by creating a classroom culture that encourages emotional expression and empathy. For example, incorporating "feelings time" into the daily routine allows children to share their emotions and practice empathy by listening to their peers. Activities like role-playing or group discussions about emotions help children understand different perspectives and develop emotional awareness.

Additionally, teachers play a key role in helping children manage conflicts and build social skills. Conflict is a natural part of group dynamics, and emotionally intelligent teachers use these moments as learning opportunities. When a disagreement arises between students, a teacher can guide them through a process of identifying their feelings, communicating effectively, and finding a resolution. This approach not only teaches conflict resolution but also reinforces the importance of empathy and emotional regulation in maintaining healthy relationships.

Caregivers, such as daycare providers or nannies, also contribute to a child's emotional intelligence, particularly in early childhood when foundational emotional skills are developed. Like parents and teachers, caregivers provide emotional support and model healthy emotional behavior. In many cases, caregivers spend a significant amount of time with children, making their role in emotional development essential. Caregivers who are attuned to a child's emotional needs can help children feel secure and understood, which fosters emotional resilience. For example, a caregiver who patiently helps a toddler navigate the frustration of sharing toys is teaching valuable lessons in emotional regulation and empathy.

Beyond individual roles, parents, teachers, and caregivers must work together to create a consistent and supportive environment for emotional development. When children receive consistent messages about emotions from all the adults in their lives, they are more likely to internalize these lessons and apply them in different settings. For instance, if both parents and teachers emphasize the importance of empathy and emotional expression, children are more likely to practice these skills at home, in school, and in social situations. Conversely, if there are conflicting messages—for example, if a parent encourages emotional expression but a teacher dismisses feelings—children may become confused or uncertain about how to handle their emotions.

The collaborative effort of parents, teachers, and caregivers is especially important in addressing emotional challenges. Children with emotional difficulties, such as anxiety, aggression, or trouble with emotional regulation, benefit most from a unified approach to emotional support. When all the adults in a child's life work together to provide consistent guidance and reinforcement of emotional skills, the child is more likely to overcome these challenges and develop healthy emotional intelligence.

In summary, parents, teachers, and caregivers each play a vital role in nurturing emotional intelligence in children. Through modeling, guidance, and support, they help children understand and manage their emotions, build empathy, and develop the social skills necessary for success. Their collaboration is key to ensuring children receive consistent and effective emotional education.

How This Book Can Help You and Your Child

This book is designed to equip parents, teachers, and caregivers with the tools and strategies needed to nurture emotional intelligence in children. By providing practical guidance, real-life examples, and evidence-based techniques, this book offers a comprehensive road map for helping children recognize and manage their emotions, develop empathy, and build healthy relationships.

One of the key ways this book can help is by breaking down the complex concept of emotional intelligence into manageable steps. Emotional intelligence might seem like an abstract idea, but with the right tools, it becomes accessible and actionable. This book offers clear, step-by-step approaches for teaching emotional skills, whether it's helping a toddler identify their emotions or guiding a teenager through the complexities of social interactions. Each chapter focuses on a specific aspect of emotional intelligence, providing strategies that can be adapted to children of all ages and developmental stages.

Additionally, this book emphasizes the importance of practical application. The goal is not just to understand emotional intelligence but to actively implement it in daily life. To this end, the book includes numerous activities, games, and exercises that parents, teachers, and caregivers can use to reinforce emotional skills. These activities are designed to be engaging and enjoyable for children, ensuring that emotional learning is both effective and fun. For example, role-playing games help children practice empathy by putting themselves in others' shoes, while mindfulness exercises teach them how to manage stress and stay calm in challenging situations.

This book also addresses common emotional challenges that children face, such as temper tantrums, sibling rivalry, peer pressure, and anxiety. By offering specific strategies for handling these situations, the book empowers adults to respond to children's emotional needs with confidence and compassion. Whether it's guiding a child through a meltdown or helping them navigate social dynamics at school, this book provides the tools necessary to tackle emotional hurdles and turn them into opportunities for growth.

What is Emotional Intelligence?

Defining Emotional Intelligence for Children

Emotional intelligence, often abbreviated as EI or EQ (emotional quotient), refers to the ability to understand, manage, and effectively use one's own emotions and to recognize and respond to the emotions of others. For children, emotional intelligence is especially important because it forms the foundation for their social development, mental health, and future success in both personal and professional realms.

Explaining emotional intelligence to children can be simplified by breaking it down into relatable concepts. One way to define it for children is by comparing emotions to a toolkit. Each tool in the emotional toolkit represents a different skill that helps them handle feelings, interact with others, and make decisions. The more tools children have in their toolkit, the better equipped they are to navigate life's ups and downs. When children understand that emotions are a normal part of life and that everyone has them, it helps demystify feelings like sadness, anger, or frustration.

Children, particularly younger ones, benefit from learning that emotional intelligence is about recognizing and naming their emotions. For example, instead of just feeling upset, children are taught to identify whether they are angry, frustrated, or disappointed. By giving a name to their feelings, children gain a sense of control over them. They also learn that emotions are not permanent; they come and go like waves in the ocean, and with the right tools, they can navigate even the stormiest emotional weather.

In addition to recognizing their own emotions, children need to understand that other people have feelings too. This awareness is key to building empathy and forming positive relationships. For example, when a child sees a friend crying, they can learn to recognize that the friend is sad and may need comfort or space. Understanding that everyone experiences emotions, and that it's okay to talk about them, encourages open communication and fosters a supportive environment where emotional intelligence can thrive.

Another important concept in defining emotional intelligence for children is the idea of emotional regulation. Children must learn that while they can't always control how they feel, they can control how they react to their emotions. This is a vital distinction that helps children avoid impulsive behavior and encourages thoughtful responses. For instance, a child who is frustrated with a difficult homework assignment might feel tempted to give up or throw a tantrum. However, with emotional intelligence, they can recognize their frustration, take a deep breath, and ask for help or take a break before trying again. Over time, this skill helps children build resilience, a critical component of emotional intelligence that allows them to bounce back from challenges.

Understanding emotional intelligence is not just about knowing what feelings are but also about developing the capacity to manage them constructively. Children who are emotionally intelligent can cope with stress, communicate their needs clearly, and collaborate effectively with others. These skills are not only crucial for their immediate well-being but also lay the groundwork for future success in school, friendships, and eventually, the workplace.

The Five Core Components (Self-awareness, Self-regulation, Motivation, Empathy, Social Skills)

Emotional intelligence can be broken down into five core components: self-awareness, self-regulation, motivation, empathy, and social skills. Each of these components plays a vital role in helping children navigate their emotional landscapes and develop strong, healthy relationships with others. Let's explore these five components in detail, focusing on how they apply to children's emotional growth and development.

Self-awareness

Self-awareness is the foundation of emotional intelligence. It involves the ability to recognize and understand one's own emotions. For children, developing self-awareness means learning to identify and name their feelings as they experience them. A self-aware child can say, "I'm feeling angry right now," or "I'm sad because my friend didn't want to play with me." This ability to label emotions is a critical first step in emotional intelligence because it allows children to begin the process of managing their feelings.

Self-awareness also involves recognizing how emotions affect behavior. Children who are self-aware understand that emotions like frustration or anger can lead to impulsive actions, such as hitting a sibling or shouting at a friend. By recognizing these emotional triggers, children can begin to take steps to manage their reactions, which is essential for emotional regulation. Additionally, self-awareness includes understanding one's strengths and weaknesses. Children who are self-aware are more likely to have a realistic sense of their abilities and limitations, which fosters confidence and encourages a growth mindset.

To nurture self-awareness in children, caregivers and educators can encourage them to reflect on their emotions and talk about how they feel. Journalism or drawing about feelings can also help younger children explore and express their emotions in a way that feels safe and manageable. The more children practice identifying and reflecting on their emotions, the more self-aware they become.

Self-regulation

Self-regulation is the ability to manage and control one's emotions, especially in challenging or stressful situations. For children, self-regulation is crucial because it helps them avoid impulsive behaviors that can lead to conflicts or problems. A child who has developed self-regulation can experience frustration, anger, or sadness without acting out inappropriately. Instead of hitting, yelling, or throwing a tantrum, a self-regulated child might take a few deep breaths, ask for help, or find a quiet space to calm down.

Teaching children self-regulation involves helping them develop strategies for managing their emotions in the moment. One common technique is teaching children to recognize the physical signs of strong emotions, such as a racing heart, clenched fists, or a hot face. These physical cues can serve as warning signs that they are about to lose control, allowing them to pause and use a calming strategy. Calming strategies for children might include deep breathing, counting to ten, or using positive self-talk. For example, a child who feels overwhelmed by a challenging task might repeat to themselves, "I can do this if I take it one step at a time."

Self-regulation also involves delayed gratification, which is the ability to resist the temptation of an immediate reward in favor of a more valuable, long-term goal. This skill is critical for children as they learn to navigate the demands of school, relationships, and future careers. For instance, a child who can resist the urge to play video games until after finishing homework demonstrates self-regulation. This ability to prioritize long-term goals over short-term pleasures is a hallmark of emotional intelligence and is strongly linked to future success in life.

Adults can help children develop self-regulation by modeling appropriate responses to stress and frustration. Children learn a great deal by observing how the adults in their lives handle their emotions. When caregivers and educators demonstrate calm, measured responses to challenges, they provide a powerful example for children to follow. Additionally, creating a predictable environment with clear rules and expectations helps children feel secure, which supports their ability to self-regulate.

Motivation

Motivation, in the context of emotional intelligence, refers to the ability to set and pursue goals, even in the face of obstacles or setbacks. Children who are motivated are not only driven by external rewards, such as praise or grades, but also by an intrinsic desire to learn, grow, and succeed. This internal motivation is a key component of emotional intelligence because it helps children persist in the face of challenges, take pride in their accomplishments, and continue striving for improvement.

For children, developing motivation begins with fostering a sense of curiosity and a love of learning. When children are motivated by their own interests and passions, they are more likely to engage deeply in activities, persevere through difficulties, and experience a sense of fulfillment from their efforts. For example, a child who loves building with Legos might spend hours constructing complex structures, even if it means facing setbacks along the way. This kind of intrinsic motivation is driven by the child's enjoyment of the process and the satisfaction of seeing a project through to completion.

Motivation is also closely tied to resilience, which is the ability to bounce back from failures or setbacks. Children who are motivated by internal goals are more likely to view challenges as opportunities for growth rather than as insurmountable obstacles. For instance, a child who fails a math test but is motivated to improve might seek help from a teacher or practice more at home, rather than giving up in frustration. This growth mindset, which focuses on effort and improvement rather than on innate ability, is a crucial part of emotional intelligence.

Adults can nurture motivation in children by offering encouragement and support, particularly when they encounter difficulties. Praising effort rather than just results helps children understand that persistence and hard work are valuable, even if success isn't immediate. Additionally, allowing children to set their own goals and take ownership of their learning fosters a sense of autonomy and intrinsic motivation. When children feel that they are in control of their own success, they are more likely to stay motivated and engaged.

Empathy

Empathy is the ability to understand and share the feelings of others. It is one of the most important components of emotional intelligence because it allows children to connect with others on a deep emotional level, fostering kindness, cooperation, and positive relationships. Empathy helps children see the world from different perspectives and respond to others with compassion, even in difficult or emotionally charged situations.

For children, developing empathy begins with recognizing that other people have feelings and that those feelings may be different from their own. This realization is the foundation of empathy and is critical for building social connections. For example, a child who sees a classmate crying because they lost a game might feel sad for their friend and offer comfort. This empathetic response helps build trust and strengthens friendships.

Empathy also involves understanding the reasons behind other people's emotions. Children who are empathetic can recognize that someone who is angry might be feeling hurt or frustrated, and that someone who is shy might feel nervous or scared. This deeper understanding of emotions allows children to respond in more thoughtful and supportive ways. For instance, instead of getting angry in return, a child might show patience and kindness toward someone who is upset, knowing that their anger might be masking another emotion.

Adults can encourage empathy in children by modeling empathetic behavior and by creating opportunities for children to practice empathy. For instance, when a child sees a friend or sibling upset, an adult can prompt the child to consider how that person might be feeling and what they could do to help. Asking questions like, "How do you think they feel right now?" or "What can we do to make them feel better?" encourages children to put themselves in someone else's shoes. Over time, these guided reflections help children internalize empathetic thinking and make it a natural part of their interactions with others.

Empathy can also be cultivated through storytelling and role-playing. Reading books or watching movies where characters experience different emotions can help children practice understanding the feelings of others. After reading a story, caregivers and educators can ask questions like, "How do you think that character felt when they were left out?" or "What would you have done in that situation?" Role-playing games where children take on different roles can also help them experience emotions from various perspectives. By stepping into someone else's shoes, even in a playful context, children gain a deeper understanding of the emotional experiences of others, which fosters greater empathy.

In a broader sense, empathy is essential for creating inclusive and compassionate communities. Children who develop empathy are more likely to engage in prosocial behaviors, such as helping others, sharing, and working collaboratively. They are also less likely to engage in bullying or exclusionary behavior, as they understand the emotional impact of such actions on others. As children grow, empathy becomes a critical skill for navigating complex social dynamics, resolving conflicts, and building meaningful relationships.

Social Skills

Social skills, the final component of emotional intelligence, refer to the ability to interact positively and effectively with others. Socially skilled children can communicate their feelings and needs clearly, listen to others, and collaborate in a way that fosters positive relationships. These skills are essential not only for making friends but also for succeeding in group settings, such as classrooms, teams, and eventually, workplaces.

For children, developing social skills begins with learning how to express themselves appropriately. This includes using "I" statements to communicate feelings ("I feel upset when you take my toy") and asking for what they need in a respectful manner. Effective communication also involves listening to others and responding in a way that acknowledges their feelings and needs. For instance, when a friend says they are upset, a socially skilled child might respond with, "I'm sorry you feel that way. Do you want to talk about it?" This kind of empathetic listening helps strengthen relationships and build trust.

Social skills also encompass cooperation and teamwork. In group settings, such as classrooms or play dates, children who have strong social skills can work collaboratively with others, share resources, and take turns. These behaviors are essential for maintaining harmony and avoiding conflicts. For example, during a group project at school, a child with strong social skills might listen to everyone's ideas, contribute their own thoughts, and help resolve disagreements in a way that benefits the entire group. This ability to work well with others is a key indicator of social competence and is highly valued in both academic and social settings.

Conflict resolution is another important aspect of social skills. No matter how emotionally intelligent a child is, conflicts will inevitably arise, whether it's over a toy, a game, or a misunderstanding. Socially skilled children know how to handle these conflicts in a constructive way. Instead of resorting to aggression or withdrawing, they can use their emotional intelligence to calm themselves, express their feelings, and work toward a solution that satisfies everyone involved. For example, if two children want to play with the same toy, a socially skilled child might suggest taking turns or finding another toy to play with together. This kind of problem-solving helps prevent conflicts from escalating and teaches children valuable negotiation and compromise skills.

To help children develop social skills, adults can provide opportunities for positive social interactions and offer guidance when conflicts arise. For example, during play dates or group activities, caregivers can facilitate cooperative games that require teamwork and communication. When disagreements occur, adults can step in to mediate, teaching children how to express their feelings, listen to others, and find a solution. Over time, these guided experiences help children build the social skills they need to navigate relationships successfully.

In addition to face-to-face interactions, social skills are becoming increasingly important in the digital age. With the rise of social media, texting, and online gaming, children are interacting with others in new ways, which presents both opportunities and challenges for social development. Socially skilled children can apply their emotional intelligence in these digital spaces, recognizing the importance of respectful communication and understanding the potential emotional impact of their words and actions online. Teaching children how to communicate effectively and em-pathetically in digital environments is a critical part of preparing them for the social challenges of the future.

In summary, social skills are the practical application of emotional intelligence in everyday interactions. They allow children to communicate effectively, resolve conflicts, and build positive relationships, both in person and online. By nurturing these skills from a young age, adults can help children develop the social competence they need to thrive in a complex and interconnected world.

Emotional intelligence, encompassing self-awareness, self-regulation, moti-vation, empathy, and social skills, is a vital aspect of a child's development. It influences how they understand and manage their own emotions, relate to others, and navigate the social world. Each of these five components contributes to a child's ability to form healthy relationships, cope with challenges, and achieve personal and academic success. By fostering emotional intelligence in children, parents, caregivers, and educators lay the foundation for a lifetime of emotional well-being and resilience. Through thoughtful guidance, role-modeling, and practice, children can develop the emotional skills they need to thrive both now and in the future.

Emotional Development in Children

Emotional Milestones from Infancy to Adolescence

Emotional development in children is a complex and dynamic process that begins in infancy and continues throughout adolescence. As children grow, their emotional capacity evolves, influenced by biological, cognitive, and social factors. Emotional milestones, or key developmental stages, are observable markers that signal a child's progress in understanding, expressing, and managing their emotions. These milestones help parents, caregivers, and educators identify typical emotional growth and provide insight into how children are developing emotionally.

In infancy, emotional development begins with basic expressions of discomfort, pleasure, or distress. Newborns communicate their emotions through crying, which is their primary way of signaling needs such as hunger, discomfort, or fatigue. Around six weeks of age, infants typically begin to smile in response to familiar faces or sounds, marking one of the first milestones in emotional development: social smiling. This social smile is not just a reflex but a sign that the infant is beginning to engage with their environment in a meaningful way. By around three months of age, infants start to express a wider range of emotions, including joy, excitement, and surprise, particularly in response to interactions with caregivers.

As infants approach six months, they develop a stronger attachment to their primary caregivers, often showing signs of preference for certain people.

This attachment is a crucial part of emotional development, as it provides the foundation for future emotional bonds. At this stage, infants may begin to exhibit stranger anxiety, showing discomfort or fear around unfamiliar people. This is a normal part of development, signaling that the infant is becoming more aware of their environment and differentiating between familiar and unfamiliar faces. By nine months, infants typically start to display more complex emotions such as anger, frustration, and fear, often in response to challenges like being separated from their caregivers or being unable to reach a desired object.

Between 12 and 18 months, toddlers experience a significant leap in emotional development as they become more mobile and independent. This period is often characterized by temper tantrums and strong emotional reactions, which are normal as toddlers struggle to regulate their emotions while asserting their independence. The development of language skills during this time also plays a crucial role in emotional expression, as toddlers begin to use words to communicate their feelings. For example, a child might say "mad" or "sad" to express their emotions, rather than relying solely on physical cues like crying or tantrums. Additionally, toddlers start to develop a sense of self-awareness, which can be observed in behaviors such as recognizing themselves in a mirror or using possessive language like "mine."

As children move into the preschool years (ages 3 to 5), their emotional development becomes more sophisticated. Preschoolers begin to understand the concept of empathy, or the ability to recognize and respond to the emotions of others. For instance, a preschooler might comfort a friend who is crying or show concern when a peer is upset. This development of empathy is closely linked to social interactions, as children at this age engage more frequently in group play and cooperative activities. Emotional regulation also improves during the preschool years, as children start to learn how to manage their emotions with the help of caregivers. For example, a child might be able to take a deep breath or seek comfort from an adult when feeling overwhelmed, rather than immediately reacting with a tantrum.

By the time children enter early elementary school (ages 6 to 8), they have a greater understanding of emotions, both their own and others'. They become more adept at reading social cues, such as facial expressions and body language, and can use this information to adjust their behavior accordingly. For instance, a child might notice that a classmate looks upset and offer a comforting word or gesture. At this stage, children also develop a stronger sense of self-esteem, which is influenced by their social interactions and successes in school. Emotional regulation continues to improve, as children learn to manage feelings like frustration or disappointment in more socially acceptable ways. For example, a child might use problem-solving skills to overcome a challenge rather than giving up or reacting with anger.

As children progress into later elementary school (ages 9 to 11), their emotional world becomes more complex. They begin to experience a wider range of emotions, including guilt, shame, and pride, and develop a greater capacity for empathy. This period is marked by an increasing ability to understand the perspectives of others, which is critical for forming deeper friendships and navigating social dynamics. Children in this age group also begin to experience more nuanced emotions, such as mixed feelings or conflicting emotions. For example, a child might feel both excited and nervous about starting a new school year, or they might feel both happy and sad about winning a game while their friend loses.

During early adolescence (ages 12 to 14), emotional development is heavily influenced by the onset of puberty, which brings about significant hormonal changes. These hormonal fluctuations can lead to intense emotional experiences, including mood swings, heightened sensitivity, and increased self-consciousness. Adolescents begin to grapple with identity formation, which includes exploring who they are, what they believe in, and how they fit into the world around them. This search for identity can lead to emotional turbulence, as adolescents may experience confusion, frustration, or anxiety about their changing bodies and social roles. Peer relationships also become increasingly important during this time, and adolescents may feel pressure to conform to social norms or worry about being accepted by their peers.

By mid-adolescence (ages 15 to 17), emotional development continues to evolve, with adolescents gaining more control over their emotional responses and a deeper understanding of their emotional experiences. They become more capable of abstract thinking, which allows them to reflect on their emotions in a more sophisticated way. For example, an adolescent might recognize that their anger stems from feelings of insecurity or that their sadness is linked to a sense of loneliness. This ability to reflect on emotions and understand their underlying causes is a key marker of emotional maturity.

Finally, in late adolescence (ages 18 to 19), individuals typically reach a level of emotional development that prepares them for adult relationships and responsibilities. They have a more stable sense of identity and a greater ability to manage their emotions in complex social situations. Emotional regulation is more advanced, allowing them to navigate challenges like romantic relationships, academic pressures, and the transition to independence with greater emotional resilience. By this stage, adolescents have developed a more nuanced understanding of emotions, both their own and others', which is critical for forming deep, meaningful connections and making decisions that align with their values and goals.

How Emotions Shape Behavior and Personality

Emotions play a critical role in shaping a child's behavior and personality. From infancy through adolescence, emotions influence how children interact with the world, how they perceive themselves, and how they respond to challenges. Understanding how emotions shape behavior and personality can help parents, caregivers, and educators support healthy emotional development and encourage positive behaviors in children.

In infancy, emotions are primarily reactive, with behaviors often serving as direct responses to emotional experiences. For example, a crying infant is likely experiencing discomfort, hunger, or distress, and their crying is a behavior that signals the need for attention or care. As infants grow, their emotional expressions become more varied and intentional, with behaviors such as smiling, reaching out, or cooing indicating pleasure, curiosity, or the desire for interaction. These early emotional behaviors help infants build attachments to caregivers and begin to explore their social environment.

As children enter the toddler years, emotions begin to have a more pronounced impact on behavior. Toddlers, who are developing a sense of independence, often experience intense emotions such as frustration or anger when they encounter obstacles or limitations. This emotional intensity is frequently expressed through behaviors like tantrums, defiance, or withdrawal. While these behaviors can be challenging for caregivers, they are also a normal part of emotional development, as toddlers learn to navigate their growing sense of autonomy. Emotional regulation skills, such as calming down after a tantrum or expressing frustration with words, are still developing at this stage, so it is common for toddlers to rely on emotional outbursts as a way of coping with overwhelming feelings.

During the preschool years, emotions continue to shape behavior in significant ways. Preschoolers are increasingly aware of social norms and expectations, and their behaviors often reflect their emotional desire to fit in with peers and please caregivers. For example, a preschooler who feels proud of a drawing may eagerly show it to a parent, seeking praise and validation. Conversely, a child who feels embarrassed or ashamed after making a mistake may hide or avoid attention. Emotional experiences during this stage contribute to the development of self-esteem and self-concept, as children begin to form beliefs about their own abilities and worth based on the emotional feedback they receive from others.

Emotions also influence social behaviors in preschoolers, as they begin to navigate friendships and group dynamics. A child who feels happy and secure is more likely to engage in cooperative play, share toys, and demonstrate prosocial behaviors like helping or comforting others. On the other hand, a child who feels anxious or excluded may exhibit behaviors such as withdrawing from play, becoming clingy with caregivers, or acting out in frustration. These early emotional experiences in social settings lay the groundwork for later social skills, such as empathy, conflict resolution, and teamwork.

In the early elementary years, emotions continue to shape behavior, but children are also becoming more adept at emotional regulation. Children in this age group are better able to manage their emotions and respond to challenges in a more measured way. For example, a child who feels frustrated with a difficult math problem may seek help from a teacher or take a break rather than immediately giving up or becoming upset. Emotional resilience begins to take root during this stage, as children learn to cope with setbacks, disappointments, and frustrations in a constructive manner.

The emotional landscape of early elementary school is also marked by the development of more complex social behaviors. Children become more aware of social hierarchies and begin to navigate peer relationships with greater sensitivity to the emotions of others. For instance, a child who feels left out from a game at recess may feel sadness or frustration, which in turn can influence their behavior. They might choose to express these feelings by seeking out a different group to play with, talking to a teacher, or in some cases, withdrawing from social interactions altogether. On the flip side, children who experience positive emotions in social settings, such as feelings of inclusion or friendship, are more likely to display prosocial behaviors like cooperation, sharing, and kindness. These social-emotional experiences play a crucial role in shaping a child's behavior, particularly in group settings, and contribute to the development of social competence.

As children progress into the later elementary school years (ages 9 to 11), emotions continue to have a profound impact on their behavior. This is a period when children begin to form a more stable sense of identity and self-concept, which is deeply influenced by their emotional experiences and the feedback they receive from others. Positive emotional experiences, such as achieving a goal in school or being praised by peers and teachers, help children develop confidence and a sense of self-worth. Conversely, negative emotional experiences, such as feeling rejected by a peer group or failing at a task, can lead to behaviors that reflect a lack of self-confidence, such as withdrawal, avoidance, or negative self-talk.

This stage also marks the beginning of more complex emotional dynamics, including the ability to experience and understand mixed emotions. For example, a child might feel both proud and nervous when presenting a project in front of the class. The ability to recognize and manage these complex emotions helps children navigate increasingly sophisticated social situations, such as group projects, friendships, and conflicts. Children at this age also begin to understand that their emotions can influence others, and they may consciously adjust their behavior based on this understanding. For instance, a child who feels upset might choose to hide their emotions in order to avoid disrupting a group activity, or they may seek out a trusted friend or adult for support.

During early adolescence (ages 12 to 14), emotions begin to play an even more significant role in shaping behavior and personality. This is a time of rapid physical, cognitive, and emotional changes, with the onset of puberty bringing about heightened emotional intensity. Adolescents often experience mood swings, emotional sensitivity, and a greater awareness of their own emotional complexity. These emotional shifts can lead to behaviors that may seem unpredictable or erratic to adults, as adolescents grapple with feelings of identity, self-worth, and belonging.

One of the defining features of early adolescence is the increased importance of peer relationships. Emotional experiences in peer settings—such as feelings of acceptance, rejection, popularity, or exclusion—can have a profound impact on behavior. Adolescents who feel accepted and valued by their peers are more likely to exhibit positive social behaviors, such as cooperation, empathy, and participation in group activities. On the other hand, adolescents who feel rejected or excluded may withdraw from social interactions, engage in attention-seeking behaviors, or act out in frustration or anger.

The search for identity is another major factor influencing behavior during adolescence. Adolescents are beginning to explore who they are, what they believe in, and how they fit into their social world. This emotional exploration often leads to behaviors that reflect an adolescent's desire to assert independence and autonomy. For example, an adolescent might challenge authority, experiment with different social groups, or adopt new interests and values. These behaviors are often driven by the emotional need to establish a sense of self, separate from parental or societal expectations. However, the emotional turbulence of adolescence can also lead to risky behaviors, such as experimenting with substances or engaging in reckless activities, particularly if the adolescent is struggling with feelings of inadequacy, loneliness, or peer pressure.

By mid-adolescence (ages 15 to 17), emotional development continues to shape behavior in significant ways, but adolescents are also beginning to gain greater control over their emotional responses. They become more adept at recognizing the causes of their emotions and can reflect on their emotional experiences in a more sophisticated way. For example, an adolescent might recognize that their feelings of anger toward a friend stem from a deeper sense of insecurity or jealousy. This ability to understand the underlying causes of emotions allows adolescents to engage in more thoughtful and reflective behavior, rather than acting impulsively in response to their feelings.

However, peer influence remains a powerful force during mid-adolescence. Adolescents who feel emotionally supported by their peer group are more likely to engage in positive behaviors, such as participating in extracurricular activities, volunteering, or pursuing academic goals. On the other hand, adolescents who feel emotionally disconnected from their peers may be more likely to engage in negative behaviors, such as skipping school, engaging in risky activities, or isolating themselves from social interactions.

As adolescents approach late adolescence (ages 18 to 19), emotional development reaches a level of maturity that prepares them for adult relationships and responsibilities. By this stage, most adolescents have developed a stable sense of identity and a greater capacity for emotional regulation. They are more capable of managing complex emotions, such as balancing the excitement of new opportunities with the anxiety of impending responsibilities (e.g., leaving home for college or starting a job). Emotional experiences during late adolescence are often closely tied to major life transitions, such as entering adulthood, forming romantic relationships, or making long-term career decisions. These emotional experiences shape behavior in profound ways, as adolescents begin to make choices that reflect their values, goals, and emotional priorities.

In terms of personality development, emotions play a central role in shaping how adolescents view themselves and interact with the world. Emotional experiences, particularly those related to relationships, successes, and failures, contribute to the formation of traits such as resilience, empathy, assertiveness, and self-confidence. For example, an adolescent who has successfully navigated challenging emotional experiences, such as overcoming a personal setback or resolving a conflict with a friend, may develop a stronger sense of resilience and self-assurance. On the other hand, an adolescent who struggles with unresolved emotional challenges, such as chronic feelings of insecurity or emotional detachment, may develop a more reserved or anxious personality.

Overall, emotions play a critical role in shaping behavior and personality throughout childhood and adolescence. From early infancy, when emotions are expressed through basic reactions like crying or smiling, to late adolescence, when emotions are deeply intertwined with identity formation and decision-making, emotional experiences influence how children and adolescents navigate their social world, respond to challenges, and develop their sense of self. Understanding the emotional milestones that mark each stage of development can help parents, caregivers, and educators provide the support and guidance needed to foster healthy emotional growth and encourage positive behaviors. As children and adolescents gain a deeper understanding of their emotions and learn to manage them effectively, they become better equipped to form meaningful relationships, pursue their goals, and develop a well-rounded, emotionally resilient personality that will serve them throughout their lives.

The Science Behind Emotional Intelligence

How the Brain Processes Emotions

Emotions are fundamental aspects of human life, driving behavior, decision-making, and social interactions. Understanding how the brain processes emotions is essential to fully grasp the science behind emotional intelligence (EI). Emotions are not isolated to one part of the brain but are the result of complex interactions between several brain regions, most notably the amygdala, the prefrontal cortex, and the hippocampus. These areas, along with neurotransmitter systems, collaborate to recognize, generate, and regulate emotional experiences.

The amygdala, a small almond-shaped structure located deep within the brain, plays a pivotal role in processing emotions, particularly those related to fear and aggression. When a person encounters an emotionally charged situation, the amygdala acts as an emotional alarm system, detecting potential threats and triggering an immediate emotional response. This response, known as the "fight-or-flight" reaction, prepares the body to deal with danger by increasing heart rate, releasing adrenaline, and enhancing sensory awareness. The amygdala processes emotional stimuli rapidly, often before the individual has a chance to consciously reflect on the situation, which is why people sometimes react instinctively in emotional situations without thinking things through.

While the amygdala is responsible for the initial emotional response, the prefrontal cortex, located at the front of the brain, plays a critical role in regulating these emotions. The prefrontal cortex is involved in higher-order thinking processes, including reasoning, decision-making, and impulse control. After the amygdala activates an emotional response, the prefrontal cortex evaluates the situation and determines whether the initial reaction is appropriate. It helps the individual to regulate their emotions, allowing them to respond to emotional stimuli in a more measured and thoughtful way. For example, if someone feels anger rising during a disagreement, the prefrontal cortex can help them suppress the urge to yell and instead suggest that they calmly explain their perspective.

This interaction between the amygdala and the prefrontal cortex is critical to emotional intelligence. Emotionally intelligent individuals have well-developed prefrontal cortices, enabling them to control impulsive emotional reactions and choose more appropriate responses to emotional situations. This ability to pause, reflect, and regulate emotional impulses is what distinguishes emotionally intelligent people from those who are more emotionally reactive.

The hippocampus, another important brain structure, is involved in forming emotional memories. Emotions and memories are deeply interconnected, as emotionally charged experiences are often more memorable than neutral ones. For example, a particularly joyful birthday party or a traumatic car accident is likely to be remembered vividly, sometimes for years. The hippocampus works with the amygdala to link emotions to memories, which is why certain smells, sounds, or images can trigger powerful emotional recollections. This process is essential for emotional learning, as it allows individuals to recall past emotional experiences and apply the lessons learned from those situations to new, similar events.

The hypothalamus also plays a role in emotional processing by regulating bodily responses to emotions. When the amygdala detects an emotional stimulus, the hypothalamus helps coordinate the physical reactions associated with emotions, such as increased heart rate, sweating, or shaking. These physical reactions are part of the body's preparation to deal with emotional or stressful situations. In cases of chronic stress or unresolved emotional distress, the hypothalamus can contribute to long-term health issues such as high blood pressure or weakened immune function due to the prolonged activation of stress responses.

In addition to these brain structures, neurotransmitters—chemical messengers in the brain—play a crucial role in regulating emotions. Serotonin is a key neurotransmitter associated with mood regulation and emotional stability. Low levels of serotonin are linked to depression, anxiety, and mood swings, while balanced serotonin levels promote feelings of well-being and emotional balance. Dopamine, another important neurotransmitter, is involved in the brain's reward system and is closely tied to feelings of pleasure, motivation, and reward. Positive emotional experiences, such as receiving praise or achieving a goal, trigger the release of dopamine, reinforcing the behavior and encouraging individuals to seek out similar experiences in the future. Dopamine imbalances, however, can lead to emotional difficulties, such as an inability to feel pleasure or motivation, commonly seen in conditions like depression.

Oxytocin, sometimes called the "love hormone," plays a vital role in social bonding and emotional connections. Released during activities like hugging, breastfeeding, or social interactions, oxytocin enhances feelings of trust, empathy, and attachment. It is particularly important in the development of emotional bonds between parents and children, as well as in romantic relationships. Oxytocin's role in emotional intelligence is evident in its ability to promote prosocial behaviors, such as cooperation, empathy, and conflict resolution, which are all key components of emotional intelligence.

The brain processes emotions through an intricate dance between these structures and chemical messengers, each contributing to the perception, expression, and regulation of emotional experiences. This process is not static; it evolves with experience and can be influenced by various factors, such as upbringing, trauma, and mental health conditions. Understanding how the brain processes emotions provides insight into why emotional intelligence varies from person to person and highlights the potential for developing and improving emotional intelligence through practice and self-awareness.

The Connection Between Emotional Intelligence and Mental Health

Emotional intelligence is closely connected to mental health, with numerous studies showing that individuals with higher levels of emotional intelligence tend to have better mental health outcomes. Emotional intelligence influences how individuals perceive and manage their emotions, which directly impacts their ability to cope with stress, anxiety, depression, and other mental health challenges.

One of the key connections between emotional intelligence and mental health lies in the ability to regulate emotions effectively. Individuals with high emotional intelligence are better equipped to handle negative emotions such as sadness, anger, or frustration. Instead of becoming overwhelmed by these feelings, they can process and manage them in healthy ways. For example, someone with high emotional intelligence might recognize that they are feeling anxious about an upcoming exam and take proactive steps to manage that anxiety, such as practicing relaxation techniques, studying in a structured way, or seeking support from a teacher or counselor. In contrast, individuals with lower emotional intelligence might struggle to regulate their emotions, leading to unhealthy coping mechanisms such as avoidance, substance abuse, or emotional outbursts.

Emotional intelligence also plays a protective role in managing stress, which is a major contributor to mental health issues. People with high emotional intelligence are more resilient in the face of stress because they are better able to recognize their emotional triggers and implement coping strategies to manage their stress levels. For example, they might use mindfulness techniques, engage in physical exercise, or talk through their feelings with a trusted friend. This emotional regulation helps prevent the buildup of chronic stress, which is linked to a range of mental health problems, including anxiety, depression, and burnout. Additionally, emotional intelligence allows individuals to identify when their stress levels are becoming unmanageable and seek help before their mental health deteriorates further.

Another important connection between emotional intelligence and mental health is the role of self-awareness. Self-awareness, one of the core components of emotional intelligence, involves recognizing and understanding one's own emotions. People with high self-awareness are more likely to notice when they are feeling mentally or emotionally unwell and take steps to address the issue. For example, someone who is feeling persistently sad or fatigued might recognize these feelings as potential signs of depression and seek professional help or make lifestyle changes to improve their mood. In contrast, individuals with low self-awareness might not recognize the signs of declining mental health until the problem has become more severe, making it harder to recover.

Emotional intelligence also enhances empathy, which is the ability to understand and share the feelings of others. Empathy is not only crucial for building strong, supportive relationships, but it also has a direct impact on mental health. Strong social connections are one of the most powerful protective factors against mental health issues, as they provide emotional support, reduce feelings of isolation, and increase a sense of belonging. People with high emotional intelligence are more likely to have positive, empathetic relationships, which can act as a buffer against stress, anxiety, and depression. In contrast, individuals who struggle with empathy may find it harder to form and maintain close relationships, leaving them more vulnerable to mental health challenges.

The connection between emotional intelligence and mental health is particularly evident in individuals with conditions like anxiety and depression. People with high emotional intelligence are less likely to experience prolonged episodes of anxiety or depression because they have the tools to manage their emotions effectively. For example, they can recognize the early signs of anxiety and implement coping strategies before it escalates into a full-blown panic attack. Similarly, they can challenge negative thought patterns that contribute to depression, replacing them with more balanced and realistic thinking. Emotional intelligence also allows individuals to express their emotions in healthy ways, such as talking to a friend or therapist, which can prevent feelings of sadness or hopelessness from spiraling into a more serious mental health issue.

Research has shown that emotional intelligence is linked to lower levels of depression and anxiety across various age groups. For instance, studies have found that emotionally intelligent adolescents are less likely to experience symptoms of anxiety and depression, likely because they are better able to manage the emotional challenges of adolescence, such as peer pressure, academic stress, and identity formation. Similarly, adults with higher emotional intelligence are more likely to experience psychological well-being, as they are better equipped to handle the emotional demands of work, relationships, and life transitions.

Emotional intelligence is also connected to self-compassion, which plays a crucial role in mental health. Self-compassion involves treating oneself with kindness and understanding during times of failure or difficulty, rather than engaging in harsh self-criticism. Individuals with high emotional intelligence are more likely to practice self-compassion, as they are better able to recognize their own emotional needs and respond to them in a nurturing way. This self-compassion helps prevent the development of negative mental health patterns, such as excessive guilt, shame, or self-blame, which are often linked to conditions like depression and anxiety. People who are emotionally intelligent tend to have a healthier internal dialogue, meaning that they can acknowledge their mistakes or challenges without being overly critical of themselves. This ability to be kind to oneself during tough times fosters resilience and helps individuals recover more quickly from setbacks, reducing the likelihood of developing long-term mental health issues.

Another significant link between emotional intelligence and mental health is its impact on emotional resilience. Resilience refers to an individual's ability to cope with adversity, stress, or trauma and bounce back from negative experiences. Emotional intelligence enhances resilience because it equips individuals with the tools needed to understand, process, and move past difficult emotions. For example, emotionally intelligent individuals can recognize when they are feeling overwhelmed by stress or grief and take steps to manage these emotions constructively. Rather than allowing these feelings to dictate their behavior or derail their daily lives, they engage in strategies that help them recover, such as seeking social support, practicing mindfulness, or focusing on problem-solving. Over time, this resilience helps protect them from the negative mental health consequences of prolonged stress or trauma.

Moreover, emotional intelligence fosters emotional expression, which is a key component of maintaining good mental health. Being able to articulate one's feelings—whether to a friend, family member, or therapist—is essential for emotional release and mental well-being. Emotional suppression, on the other hand, has been linked to increased stress, anxiety, and even physical health problems. People with high emotional intelligence are better able to communicate their emotions in appropriate and effective ways, allowing them to work through their emotional challenges rather than bottling them up. For instance, someone who is going through a difficult time might openly express their feelings of sadness or frustration to a close friend, which can lead to emotional relief and support. This expression of emotions not only alleviates mental strain but also strengthens relationships by fostering understanding and empathy from others.

In the context of social and romantic relationships, emotional intelligence plays a crucial role in mental health. Emotionally intelligent individuals are more likely to build and maintain healthy relationships, which serve as a critical support system for mental well-being. Positive relationships provide emotional comfort, practical support, and a sense of belonging, all of which are important protective factors against mental health problems. Conversely, individuals with low emotional intelligence may struggle to navigate the complexities of relationships, leading to misunderstandings, conflicts, and emotional isolation. This can result in feelings of loneliness or frustration, which are closely linked to mental health issues such as depression. Therefore, developing emotional intelligence not only improves individual emotional regulation but also contributes to stronger, more supportive social connections that enhance overall mental health.

Furthermore, emotional intelligence is linked to psychological flexibility, which refers to the ability to adapt one's thinking and behavior in response to changing circumstances or challenges. Psychological flexibility is critical for mental health because it allows individuals to approach problems with an open mind, adjust their strategies when needed, and avoid rigid thinking patterns that can exacerbate stress or anxiety. People with high emotional intelligence tend to be more psychologically flexible, as they are better able to assess their emotions and respond to situations in a balanced and thoughtful way. For instance, an emotionally intelligent person facing a career setback may initially feel disappointed, but rather than dwelling on these feelings, they can adapt their mindset, focus on what they can control, and move forward with a new plan. This adaptability reduces the likelihood of falling into negative thought cycles that can lead to mental health challenges.

Trauma and emotional intelligence are also closely linked. Emotional intelligence can play a protective role for individuals who have experienced trauma, helping them process their emotions in healthier ways. Trauma survivors with high emotional intelligence may be better equipped to manage the emotional fallout of their experiences, as they can recognize and validate their feelings, seek appropriate support, and avoid maladaptive coping mechanisms such as emotional suppression or substance use. Furthermore, emotionally intelligent trauma survivors are often more capable of building strong social support networks, which are crucial for healing and mental health recovery. On the other hand, individuals with lower emotional intelligence may struggle to process their emotions after trauma, increasing their risk for mental health conditions such as post-traumatic stress disorder (PTSD), depression, and anxiety.

Mindfulness and emotional intelligence are two interconnected concepts that significantly impact mental health. Mindfulness involves paying attention to the present moment with curiosity and without judgment, which helps individuals become more aware of their emotions and thoughts. Practicing mindfulness can enhance emotional intelligence by increasing self-awareness and improving emotion regulation. For example, someone who practices mindfulness may be better able to notice when they are feeling stressed or overwhelmed and take proactive steps to calm themselves down. This awareness allows them to manage their emotional responses more effectively, reducing the impact of stress on their mental health. Research has shown that mindfulness practices, such as meditation or deep breathing, can improve emotional intelligence by promoting greater emotional balance and reducing reactivity, which in turn enhances mental well-being.

Lastly, emotional intelligence also plays a critical role in workplace mental health. In professional environments, emotionally intelligent individuals are more likely to experience job satisfaction, reduced stress, and better overall mental health. This is because emotional intelligence helps individuals navigate the complexities of workplace relationships, manage work-related stress, and maintain a positive work-life balance. For example, an emotion-ally intelligent employee is more likely to handle criticism constructively, collaborate effectively with colleagues, and manage their workload in a way that prevents burnout. On the other hand, individuals with lower emotional intelligence may struggle with the emotional demands of the workplace, leading to higher levels of stress, frustration, and mental exhaustion. Over time, these challenges can contribute to mental health issues such as burnout, anxiety, or depression.

In conclusion, the connection between emotional intelligence and mental health is profound and multifaceted. Emotional intelligence provides individuals with the tools to recognize, regulate, and express their emotions in healthy ways, which enhances their ability to cope with stress, build positive relationships, and maintain mental well-being. People with higher emotional intelligence are more likely to experience resilience, emotional stability, and psychological flexibility, all of which are protective factors against mental health issues. By fostering emotional intelligence through practices such as mindfulness, self-awareness, and empathy, individuals can not only improve their emotional regulation but also safeguard their mental health in the long term.

Helping Children Identify Their Emotions

The Language of Feelings: Words Children Can Use to Express Emotions

One of the most important aspects of emotional development in children is helping them build a robust vocabulary to express their feelings. Emotions can be overwhelming, especially for children who may not yet understand what they are feeling or how to articulate it. By teaching children the language of feelings, we empower them to communicate more effectively, fostering emotional intelligence and helping them to navigate their social and internal worlds more confidently.

The ability to label emotions is often referred to as "emotional literacy." Just as literacy in reading and writing involves the ability to decode symbols and words, emotional literacy requires the ability to identify and describe emotions with words. Without the proper vocabulary, children may struggle to express their feelings, leading to frustration, behavioral issues, or withdrawal. For example, a child who cannot articulate that they are feeling frustrated may resort to crying or acting out in anger because they lack the words to express their inner experience.

To cultivate emotional literacy, it is essential to introduce children to a wide range of words that describe different emotions. Basic emotions such as happiness, sadness, anger, and fear are often the starting point for this education. However, as children grow, it is important to expand their vocabulary to include more nuanced emotions such as frustration, embarrassment, excitement, jealousy, and pride. The more specific and varied a child's emotional vocabulary, the better equipped they will be to understand and communicate their feelings.

Teaching the language of feelings begins with helping children understand that emotions are a normal and natural part of life. Parents, caregivers, and educators can model this by naming their own emotions in everyday situations. For example, a parent might say, "I'm feeling really proud of you for working so hard on your homework" or "I'm feeling a little frustrated because I can't find my keys." This kind of language not only normalizes emotional expression but also provides children with concrete examples of how to use emotion words in context.

For younger children, visual aids can be an effective tool for teaching emotional vocabulary. Emotion charts or "feeling faces" posters are commonly used in classrooms and at home to help children associate facial expressions with specific emotions. These charts typically depict simple, exaggerated facial expressions—such as a smiling face for happiness or a frowning face for sadness—alongside corresponding emotion words. By referring to these charts, children can begin to make connections between what they are feeling and the appropriate words to describe those feelings.

Storybooks are another powerful tool for introducing children to the language of emotions. Many children's books focus on characters who experience a range of emotions, providing opportunities for children to see how different feelings are expressed and managed. After reading a story, parents or teachers can ask questions like, "How do you think the character felt when that happened?" or "Have you ever felt like that before?" These discussions encourage children to reflect on their own emotions and practice using emotional vocabulary.

As children develop their emotional vocabulary, it is important to encourage them to use these words in their daily lives. For instance, when a child seems upset, a parent might ask, "Are you feeling sad or frustrated right now?" Offering these emotion words gives the child the opportunity to label their feelings accurately. Over time, this practice helps children become more comfortable identifying and expressing their emotions in a variety of situations, which is essential for healthy emotional development.

It is also crucial to teach children that emotions can be mixed or layered. While young children often experience emotions in a black-and-white way—feeling either happy or sad, angry or calm—older children can begin to understand that they may feel multiple emotions at once. For example, a child might feel both excited and nervous about starting a new school year, or they might feel both proud and embarrassed after giving a presentation in front of the class. By introducing words like "conflicted," "unsure," or "bittersweet," we help children recognize and articulate these more complex emotional experiences.

In addition to teaching children to label their own emotions, it is equally important to help them develop the language to recognize and respond to the emotions of others. This is a crucial aspect of empathy and social-emotional learning. Children can learn phrases like, "It seems like you're feeling upset. Is there something I can do to help?" or "I see that you're feeling really excited about this!" These kinds of statements demonstrate emotional awareness and help children build stronger, more empathetic relationships with their peers.

Ultimately, helping children identify their emotions and giving them the language to express those emotions fosters emotional intelligence. Children who can articulate their feelings are more likely to seek help when they need it, resolve conflicts peacefully, and build healthy relationships. As they grow, this ability to understand and express emotions will serve them in all areas of life, from academic success to personal well-being.

Tools for Teaching Emotional Vocabulary

Teaching children to recognize and name their emotions requires a thoughtful approach, with a variety of tools and techniques that cater to different developmental stages. These tools not only help children build their emotional vocabulary but also support their ability to express emotions in healthy, constructive ways. Here are some of the most effective tools for teaching emotional vocabulary:

1. Emotion Cards and Charts

Emotion cards and charts are visual aids that depict different feelings through facial expressions, colors, or symbols. These tools are particularly effective for younger children who may not yet have the verbal skills to describe their emotions in words. By associating visual cues with specific emotions, children can begin to make connections between what they are feeling and the appropriate words to describe those feelings.

For example, a set of emotion cards might feature pictures of cartoon characters with various facial expressions, such as a smiling character for "happy" or a scowling character for "angry." Children can use these cards to point to the emotion they are experiencing, which helps them practice identifying and labeling their feelings. Over time, as their emotional vocabulary grows, they will become more comfortable using words to describe their emotions.

Emotion charts are similar to emotion cards but are typically displayed in classrooms or at home. These charts often include a range of emotions, from basic feelings like "happy" and "sad" to more complex emotions like "frustrated" or "embarrassed." Children can refer to the chart when they are having trouble identifying their emotions, making it a useful tool for self-reflection.

2. Emotion Wheels

An emotion wheel is a circular chart that displays a wide variety of emotions arranged in categories or levels of intensity. The center of the wheel typically contains basic emotions, such as happiness or anger, while the outer rings feature more nuanced emotions, such as "elated" or "enraged." Emotion wheels are useful for older children who have already mastered basic emotional vocabulary and are ready to explore more specific and complex emotions.

For example, a child might start by identifying that they feel angry. By referring to the emotion wheel, they can then pinpoint whether they are mildly irritated, extremely furious, or somewhere in between. This tool helps children move beyond broad emotion categories and become more precise in describing their feelings, which can lead to better emotional self-awareness and communication.

3. Storytelling and Role-Playing

Stories and role-playing scenarios provide excellent opportunities for children to explore emotions and practice using emotional vocabulary. When children engage with stories—whether through books, movies, or imaginative play—they encounter characters who experience a range of emotions. Discussing these emotions in the context of the story helps children practice identifying feelings in themselves and others.

For instance, after reading a story about a character who overcomes a challenge, parents or teachers can ask questions like, "How do you think the character felt when they faced that obstacle?" or "Have you ever felt proud like the character did when they succeeded?" These questions prompt children to reflect on emotions and articulate them in words, reinforcing their emotional vocabulary.

Role-playing allows children to act out different emotional scenarios, giving them the chance to practice identifying and expressing emotions in real-time.

For example, a parent might pretend to be a friend who is feeling sad, while the child practices offering comfort and asking about the friend's feelings. This type of play helps children develop empathy and enhances their ability to respond appropriately to the emotions of others.

4. Journalism and Drawing

For older children, journalism can be a valuable tool for exploring emotions and expanding emotional vocabulary. By writing about their feelings, children practice putting their emotions into words, which can lead to greater emotional awareness and clarity. Journalism also provides a safe, private space for children to reflect on difficult or confusing emotions without the pressure of immediate social interaction.

Children who may not yet be comfortable with written language can express their emotions through drawing. For example, a child might draw a picture of themselves feeling angry or sad, using colors and shapes to represent their emotions. Afterward, they can describe their drawing to a parent or teacher, providing an opportunity to practice using emotional vocabulary in a creative and non-threatening way.

5. Emotion Scales

Emotion scales help children quantify the intensity of their emotions, making it easier for them to communicate how they are feeling. These scales often use a simple 1 to 5 or 1 to 10 rating system, with 1 representing mild emotions and 5 or 10 representing very strong emotions. For instance, a child who is feeling frustrated might rate their frustration as a "2" if they are only mildly irritated, or a "5" if they are extremely upset.

Emotion scales can be useful in situations where children may have trouble explaining the intensity of their emotions verbally. By assigning a number to their feelings, they can communicate more effectively with parents, teachers, or peers about what they are experiencing. This tool also helps children practice emotional regulation, as they learn to monitor the intensity of their emotions and take steps to manage them before they escalate.

6. Music and Movement

Music and movement provide another avenue for children to explore and express their emotions. Certain types of music can evoke specific emotional responses in children, allowing them to connect their internal emotional state with external stimuli. For example, upbeat, fast-paced music might evoke feelings of excitement or joy, while slower, more somber music can help children identify feelings of sadness or calm. After listening to a piece of music, parents or teachers can encourage children to describe how it made them feel, asking questions like, "Did this song make you feel happy or relaxed?" or "What do you think the music sounds like—does it feel fast and excited, or slow and peaceful?"

Movement, such as dancing or acting out emotions with the body, can also help children express feelings that they may not yet be able to verbalize. For instance, a child might stomp their feet to express anger or spin in circles to show happiness. These physical actions help children release emotional energy while also making connections between their internal emotional experiences and external expression. Once they have acted out the emotions, caregivers can follow up by helping the child label what they were expressing, reinforcing emotional vocabulary.

7. Games and Interactive Apps

Interactive games and apps designed to teach emotional vocabulary can make learning about emotions fun and engaging for children. These tools often include activities where children are asked to identify different emotions based on facial expressions, scenarios, or verbal cues. For example, a game might show a series of faces and ask the child to match the correct emotion word with each face, such as "happy," "angry," or "surprised." Other games might present children with different social scenarios and ask them how they would feel in that situation or how they think others might feel.

Many educational apps are designed specifically to help children improve their emotional literacy. These apps use interactive elements like puzzles, quizzes, and storytelling to reinforce emotional vocabulary while providing real-time feedback. By making the process of learning about emotions interactive and enjoyable, games and apps encourage children to practice emotional identification and expression in a low-pressure environment.

8. Mindfulness and Breathing Exercises

Mindfulness and breathing exercises can also be valuable tools for helping children become more aware of their emotions. Mindfulness encourages children to focus on the present moment, including their thoughts, bodily sensations, and feelings. By guiding children to tune into their emotions without judgment, mindfulness practices can help them recognize and label what they are feeling more accurately. For example, a child might be encouraged to sit quietly and notice where they feel tension in their body when they are upset, such as tightness in their stomach or shoulders. Afterward, they can be asked to describe the emotions that might be causing those physical sensations.

Breathing exercises can be particularly helpful for children who are feeling overwhelmed by strong emotions like anger or anxiety. By focusing on their breath, children can calm their bodies and minds, which makes it easier for them to reflect on and identify their emotions. Once they are in a calmer state, they can use their emotional vocabulary to describe how they were feeling before and after the exercise. This process not only helps children practice emotion regulation but also reinforces the connection between physical sensations and emotional states.

9. Emotion Journals

An emotion journal is another tool that can be introduced to children, especially those who are beginning to write independently. The purpose of an emotion journal is to provide a private space where children can track their feelings over time. The journal might include prompts such as "Today, I felt…" or "When I was playing with my friend, I felt…" These prompts encourage children to reflect on their daily emotional experiences and put their feelings into words.

Emotion journals can be particularly useful for children who are learning to recognize patterns in their emotional experiences. For example, they might notice that they feel anxious every morning before school or that they feel happy when they spend time with a particular friend. Recognizing these patterns helps children develop a deeper understanding of their emotional responses and how different situations influence their feelings. Parents and teachers can periodically review the journal with the child to discuss any recurring emotions and offer support or strategies for managing difficult feelings.

10. Emotion-Based Questioning

Parents, caregivers, and educators can also use emotion-based questioning to help children develop their emotional vocabulary. This strategy involves asking children specific questions about their emotions, encouraging them to reflect on how they feel and why. For example, after a child experiences a conflict with a peer, a parent might ask, "How did that make you feel?" or "What do you think your friend was feeling?" These questions prompt the child to pause and consider their emotions in relation to the situation, which helps build emotional awareness.

Emotion-based questioning can also be used proactively to help children anticipate their emotions in future situations. For instance, before a child starts a new activity or attends a social event, a caregiver might ask, "How do you think you'll feel when you try this new thing?" or "Are you feeling nervous or excited about meeting new people?" Encouraging children to think about their emotions in advance helps them prepare for the emotional challenges they might face and equips them with the vocabulary to express their feelings as they arise.

11. Modeling Emotional Expression

Perhaps one of the most powerful tools for teaching emotional vocabulary is modeling. Children learn a great deal about emotional expression by observing the adults around them. When parents, caregivers, and teachers openly express their emotions in healthy, constructive ways, children are more likely to mirror these behaviors. For example, if a parent openly discusses their feelings of frustration after a difficult day at work and explains how they managed those emotions, the child learns that it is okay to express negative emotions and that there are effective strategies for handling them.

Modeling emotional expression involves not only sharing one's own emotions but also using emotional vocabulary to describe the emotions of others. For example, during a conversation about a character in a story or a family member's recent experience, a parent might say, "I think Grandma was feeling sad when we left her house because she misses us." This type of language helps children understand that emotions are a natural part of human relationships and that it is important to acknowledge and discuss them openly.

12. Social Stories

Social stories are short narratives that describe specific social situations and the emotions that might arise in those scenarios. These stories are often used with young children or children who have difficulty understanding social cues, such as those with autism. A social story might explain what happens during a birthday party, for example, and describe how different people might feel during the event—happiness while opening presents, nervousness while meeting new friends, or sadness when the party ends.

By reading and discussing social stories, children can practice identifying emotions in context and predicting how they might feel in similar situations. Social stories also provide examples of how to handle different emotional experiences, such as using calming strategies when feeling overwhelmed or expressing gratitude when receiving a gift. These narratives give children a framework for understanding and managing their emotions in real-life social interactions.

By using these tools, parents, caregivers, and educators can help children build a rich emotional vocabulary and develop the skills they need to identify, understand, and express their feelings. Teaching children to recognize and name their emotions is a foundational step in promoting emotional intelligence, which is essential for their social development, mental health, and overall well-being. As children become more comfortable with the language of feelings, they gain the ability to communicate their needs more effectively, navigate social relationships with greater empathy, and manage their emotions in healthy, constructive ways. This emotional literacy will serve them throughout their lives, equipping them to face challenges, build strong connections with others, and maintain emotional resilience in the face of adversity.

Understanding and Validating a Child's Emotions

Why It's Important to Acknowledge Their Feelings

Acknowledging a child's feelings is one of the most critical components of healthy emotional development. When a child's emotions are recognized and validated, they feel seen, understood, and valued, which fosters a sense of security and confidence in their emotional world. Ignoring or dismissing a child's emotions can lead to frustration, confusion, and emotional insecurity, which can have long-term impacts on their mental health and social interactions.

Children are often in the early stages of understanding their own emotions, and they rely heavily on the adults around them to help them make sense of what they are feeling. When parents, caregivers, or educators acknowledge a child's emotions, they send the message that feelings are important and worth exploring. This acknowledgment not only helps the child feel connected to their caregivers but also teaches them that it's okay to have emotions, even difficult ones, and that emotions can be managed in healthy ways.

One of the key reasons it is important to acknowledge a child's feelings is that it fosters emotional literacy. Emotional literacy, or the ability to recognize, understand, and communicate emotions, is foundational to emotional intelligence. When a caregiver validates a child's emotions, they are effectively modeling how to identify and express feelings. For example, if a child is upset after being left out of a game at recess, a caregiver might say, "I can see you're feeling sad because your friends didn't include you. That must have been hard." This kind of validation helps the child put words to their feelings, making it easier for them to understand their emotional experience and communicate it to others in the future.

Acknowledging emotions also supports a child's self-esteem and sense of worth. When a child's feelings are validated, they learn that their emotions matter and that their experiences are important. This builds a sense of self-worth and encourages the child to trust their own emotional experiences. In contrast, when a child's emotions are dismissed or minimized—such as when a caregiver says, "You're overreacting" or "It's not that big of a deal"—the child may begin to question their feelings or feel that their emotions are unimportant. Over time, this can lead to emotional insecurity and a reluctance to share their feelings, which can negatively impact their relationships and mental health.

Children who are regularly acknowledged and validated are more likely to develop emotional resilience, the ability to cope with stress and bounce back from adversity. This is because they learn that emotions, even difficult ones like sadness, anger, or frustration, are temporary and manageable. When a caregiver validates a child's feelings, they help the child see that it's okay to feel upset and that these feelings can be worked through. For instance, if a child is feeling angry because they lost a game, a parent might say, "I understand why you're upset. Losing can be frustrating. Would you like to talk about it?" This response acknowledges the child's feelings without minimizing them, which encourages the child to process their emotions rather than suppress them.

Validating a child's emotions also strengthens the parent-child bond. When caregivers consistently recognize and validate their child's feelings, they build a relationship based on trust, empathy, and open communication. The child learns that their caregivers are a safe and supportive resource, someone they can turn to when they are feeling overwhelmed or confused. This secure emotional connection is vital for a child's overall well-being and helps establish a strong foundation for healthy relationships throughout their life.

Moreover, acknowledging a child's feelings teaches them empathy. When a caregiver models empathy by validating the child's emotions, the child learns how to apply that empathy in their own interactions with others. For example, when a parent says, "I can see why you're feeling sad because your friend didn't want to play today," the child not only feels understood but also learns how to recognize and empathize with the emotions of others. This ability to understand and respond to the emotions of others is a key component of emotional intelligence and is critical for building strong, supportive relationships.

In contrast, when children's emotions are routinely dismissed or invalidated, they may develop a sense of emotional disconnection or confusion. If a child's feelings are consistently minimized, they may start to believe that their emotions are not valid or that they should suppress their feelings. This can lead to emotional detachment, where the child shuts down emotionally in an attempt to avoid feeling vulnerable or rejected. Over time, this can contribute to emotional regulation difficulties, anxiety, or depression, as the child struggles to manage their internal emotional experiences without support or validation.

In addition to the psychological benefits, acknowledging and validating a child's emotions can also lead to improved behavior. Children who feel understood and validated are more likely to cooperate and communicate openly, while children who feel dismissed or ignored may act out in frustration or resort to tantrums as a way of expressing their unmet emotional needs. For instance, if a child's frustration is dismissed during a difficult homework assignment, they may become increasingly upset, leading to a tantrum. On the other hand, if a caregiver acknowledges the child's frustration and offers support, the child is more likely to calm down and engage with the task.

In summary, acknowledging a child's feelings is crucial for their emotional development, self-esteem, and overall mental health. It helps them build emotional literacy, fosters emotional resilience, and strengthens the parent-child bond. By validating a child's emotions, caregivers teach them that their feelings are important and worth addressing, laying the foundation for healthy emotional regulation and positive social interactions throughout their life.

Strategies for Active Listening and Validation

Active listening and validation are two essential strategies for helping children feel understood, valued, and emotionally supported. When children experience strong emotions, they need to know that the adults in their lives are present, attentive, and genuinely interested in what they are feeling. By actively listening to a child and validating their emotions, caregivers can create an environment where the child feels safe to express their feelings and work through emotional challenges.

Active listening involves giving a child your full attention, both verbally and non-verbally, while they are expressing their emotions. It requires being fully present in the moment, avoiding distractions, and making a conscious effort to understand what the child is trying to communicate. When a caregiver practices active listening, they send the message that the child's feelings are important and worth paying attention to.

One of the first steps in active listening is to create a conducive environment for emotional expression. This means finding a quiet, comfortable space where the child can feel safe to share their feelings without interruptions or distractions. For example, if a child comes home from school feeling upset, it may be helpful to sit down with them in a calm setting, away from the noise of the television or other family members, to have a focused conversation. Creating this kind of environment signals to the child that their emotions are a priority and that their caregiver is ready to listen attentively.

Eye contact and body language are also crucial elements of active listening. When a caregiver makes eye contact and faces the child, it shows that they are fully engaged in the conversation and paying attention to what the child is saying. Open, relaxed body language—such as leaning slightly forward or nodding in response to the child's words—can help convey empathy and understanding. In contrast, distracted behaviors like checking a phone or looking away can signal to the child that their emotions are not being taken seriously, which may discourage them from sharing their feelings in the future.

Another important component of active listening is reflective listening, which involves repeating or paraphrasing what the child has said to demonstrate understanding. For example, if a child says, "I'm really mad because my friend didn't play with me today," the caregiver might respond by saying, "It sounds like you're feeling hurt and angry because your friend didn't want to play. That must have been hard." This type of reflection not only reassures the child that their emotions are being heard but also helps them clarify their feelings. Reflective listening can also encourage further conversation, as it invites the child to expand on what they are feeling and why.

In addition to reflective listening, open-ended questions can help the child explore their emotions more deeply. Rather than asking yes or no questions, caregivers can use questions that encourage the child to describe their feelings and experiences in greater detail. For instance, instead of asking, "Are you mad?" a caregiver might ask, "Can you tell me more about what happened with your friend?" or "How did that make you feel when they didn't include you?" Open-ended questions give the child space to articulate their emotions in their own words and offer more opportunities for the caregiver to validate their experience.

Empathetic statements are another effective strategy for validating a child's emotions. Empathy involves putting yourself in the child's shoes and responding to their emotions with understanding and compassion. An empathetic statement acknowledges the child's feelings without judgment or dismissal. For example, if a child is feeling scared about going to the doctor, a parent might say, "I understand that you're feeling scared. It's okay to feel that way. Going to the doctor can be a little scary, but I'll be with you the whole time." This response validates the child's fear while also offering reassurance and support.

In contrast, invalidating responses—such as telling a child they are over-reacting, minimizing their feelings, or offering a solution without first acknowledging their emotions—can leave the child feeling misunderstood or dismissed. For instance, saying "Don't be silly, it's just a doctor's visit" may dismiss the child's fear and discourage them from sharing their emotions in the future. Even well-meaning attempts to fix the problem immediately, such as saying "It'll be fine, don't worry about it," can sometimes bypass the important step of validating the child's emotions. Children need to feel that their emotions are recognized before they can move on to problem-solving or reassurance. Validation acknowledges the child's emotional experience and communicates that their feelings are legitimate, even if the situation may seem minor or temporary from an adult's perspective.

Another key strategy in active listening and validation is using validating language that conveys acceptance of the child's emotions. This language helps the child feel that their emotions are understandable and that it's okay to feel the way they do. Statements such as "I can see that you're really upset right now," or "It's completely normal to feel angry in this situation," validate the child's emotions without trying to change them or make them go away. Validation does not mean agreeing with the child's perspective if their emotional response seems out of proportion, but it does mean acknowledging that their emotions are real and significant to them at that moment.

A crucial aspect of validation is recognizing the child's emotional needs and allowing them space to express those needs without judgment or interruption. Sometimes children just need to vent their feelings without looking for immediate solutions or advice. In these moments, caregivers should resist the urge to jump in with advice or solutions and instead focus on being present and attentive. A simple, "I'm here to listen," or "It sounds like you're really upset, and that's okay," can go a long way in helping the child feel supported and understood. By doing this, caregivers also teach children that they don't have to fix every emotional problem immediately—that sometimes, just sitting with difficult emotions is part of the process.

Once a child's emotions have been validated, caregivers can help guide them toward emotional regulation and problem-solving. This step should only come after the child has had the chance to express their emotions fully and feel understood. For example, if a child is upset about a conflict with a sibling, the caregiver might first acknowledge their feelings by saying, "It sounds like you're really frustrated with your brother right now." Once the child feels validated, the caregiver can then help them think through possible solutions: "What do you think might help you feel better? Would you like to take a break or talk it through with your brother?"

Helping children identify coping strategies for managing their emotions is another important part of the validation process. After acknowledging the child's feelings, caregivers can work with the child to find healthy ways to cope with those emotions, whether it's through deep breathing, taking a walk, or talking to someone they trust. This process not only helps the child manage their immediate emotional response but also teaches them long-term strategies for emotional regulation that they can use in the future.

Additionally, emotional labeling is an important tool for validation, especially with younger children who may not yet have the language to describe their emotions. By naming the emotion for the child, caregivers provide them with the vocabulary to better understand and communicate their feelings. For instance, a caregiver might say, "It looks like you're feeling really frustrated because your toy broke. That's tough." Labeling emotions helps children develop emotional literacy and reinforces the idea that it's normal to have a range of feelings.

Timing is also essential when it comes to validating emotions. Sometimes, children need immediate validation, especially if they are in the midst of a strong emotional reaction, such as a tantrum or crying. In these moments, trying to explain or rationalize the situation may not be effective. Instead, caregivers can focus on calming the child and validating their emotions: "I can see that you're really upset right now, and that's okay. Let's take a few deep breaths together." Once the child has calmed down, there may be more space for discussing the situation or finding a solution. At other times, children may need time to process their emotions before they are ready to talk. In these cases, it's important for caregivers to remain patient and available when the child is ready to open up.

It's also worth noting that cultural context can play a role in how emotions are validated. Different cultures have different norms around emotional expression, and caregivers should be mindful of these when validating a child's emotions. For example, in some cultures, direct expressions of anger or sadness may be discouraged, while in others, emotional expression may be encouraged and celebrated. Caregivers can support a child's emotional development by validating their feelings in a way that respects cultural norms while also promoting healthy emotional expression.

Ultimately, validating a child's emotions through active listening and empathetic responses not only helps the child feel understood but also teaches them important skills for managing their own emotions and relating to others. When children learn that their feelings are valid and that they can talk about them openly, they are more likely to develop into emotionally healthy and resilient individuals.

Teaching Empathy Early On

Encouraging Compassion and Understanding in Young Children

Teaching empathy to children is one of the most vital aspects of their emotional and social development. Empathy, which is the ability to understand and share the feelings of others, plays a critical role in building healthy relationships, fostering compassion, and promoting emotional intelligence. When children learn to empathize, they are better equipped to navigate social dynamics, resolve conflicts, and engage in prosocial behaviors that benefit both themselves and their communities.

Empathy does not develop overnight. It is a skill that needs to be nurtured from an early age, with children gradually learning to move from a self-centered understanding of the world to recognizing the perspectives and emotions of others. For very young children, the world revolves around their immediate needs and experiences. As they grow, however, they begin to develop a broader awareness of the emotions and experiences of those around them. Encouraging empathy early on lays the groundwork for children to become compassionate, socially responsible individuals who can form strong, supportive relationships throughout their lives.

The foundation of empathy starts with emotional literacy—the ability to identify and name emotions, both in oneself and in others. Before children can empathize with others, they need to be able to recognize and understand their own emotions. When caregivers help children label their feelings ("I can see you're feeling sad because your toy broke"), they are teaching emotional awareness. This emotional literacy enables children to later apply the same understanding to others' emotions. Children who can identify when they are feeling angry, sad, or happy are better able to recognize and respond to those emotions in others.

Encouraging empathy in children also requires modeling from caregivers and educators. Children learn a great deal from observing the behavior of the adults around them. When caregivers consistently show empathy in their own interactions—whether it's comforting a friend, offering help to someone in need, or simply acknowledging someone's feelings—children absorb these behaviors and are more likely to mimic them. For example, if a parent or teacher sees another child crying and responds by saying, "It looks like you're feeling really upset. Is there anything I can do to help?" they are demonstrating empathy. This kind of modeling shows children how to recognize emotions in others and respond with compassion.

It is important to normalize conversations about emotions in the home and classroom. When caregivers create an environment where feelings are openly discussed and validated, children learn that emotions are a natural and important part of life. This normalization helps children become more comfortable with their own feelings and more attuned to the emotions of others. For example, if a parent regularly asks their child, "How are you feeling today?" or "How did that make you feel?" the child learns that it's not only acceptable to talk about emotions but also important to consider how others might be feeling in similar situations.

Storytelling is another powerful tool for encouraging empathy in young children. Stories, whether they are read from books or shared orally, allow children to step into the shoes of different characters and experience emotions from new perspectives. Through stories, children can explore complex emotions and relationships in a safe, engaging way. For example, a story about a character who feels left out or who overcomes a challenge can prompt discussions about how the character felt and how the child might have responded in a similar situation. Asking questions like, "How do you think that character felt when they were left out?" or "What could the other characters have done to help?" encourages children to reflect on emotions and consider how their actions might affect others.

Additionally, praise and positive reinforcement play a critical role in encouraging empathy in young children. When caregivers acknowledge and praise empathetic behavior, children are more likely to repeat those behaviors in the future. For instance, if a child comforts a friend who is upset, a caregiver might say, "That was very kind of you to help your friend when they were feeling sad. You really made them feel better." This kind of reinforcement helps children associate empathy with positive outcomes and encourages them to continue showing compassion in their interactions with others.

Perspective-taking is a key element of empathy, and teaching children to see things from another person's point of view is essential in fostering understanding. While very young children are naturally egocentric—meaning they see the world primarily from their own perspective—they gradually develop the ability to understand that others may have different thoughts, feelings, and experiences. Encouraging children to practice perspective-taking can be as simple as asking questions like, "How do you think your friend felt when that happened?" or "What do you think it's like for them right now?" These kinds of questions help children step outside of their own experience and imagine what it might be like for someone else.

Teaching empathy also involves helping children recognize the consequences of their actions on others. When a child sees how their behavior affects those around them, they are more likely to make choices that are compassionate and considerate. For example, if a child teases a classmate and the classmate becomes upset, a teacher might explain, "When you said that, it hurt their feelings. How do you think you would feel if someone said that to you?" This kind of feedback helps children understand the emotional impact of their actions and encourages them to be more mindful in the future.

It's also important to create opportunities for cooperative play and group activities, as these interactions naturally promote empathy by requiring children to work together, share, and resolve conflicts. Activities that involve collaboration, such as building something together or playing a team game, encourage children to consider the feelings and needs of others. For example, if two children are working on a puzzle together and one child becomes frustrated, the other child might offer encouragement or suggest a new strategy. These kinds of cooperative experiences help children practice empathy in real-world situations.

Additionally, emotional regulation is closely tied to empathy. Children who are able to manage their own emotions are better equipped to empathize with others. When a child is overwhelmed by their own emotions, it can be difficult for them to focus on how someone else might be feeling. Therefore, teaching children how to regulate their emotions—through strategies like deep breathing, counting to ten, or taking a break—can support their ability to empathize. Once children have calmed their own emotions, they are in a better position to consider the emotions of others and respond with empathy.

Finally, it's important to encourage diversity and inclusivity when teaching empathy. Children should be exposed to a wide range of experiences, cultures, and perspectives to help them develop a deeper understanding of the world and the people in it. Reading books that feature diverse characters, discussing different cultural practices, and encouraging curiosity about other people's experiences all help children expand their empathy. When children are encouraged to see the world from multiple perspectives, they are more likely to develop a broad sense of empathy that extends beyond their immediate environment.

Activities to Help Kids Relate to Others' Feelings

There are numerous activities that caregivers and educators can use to help children practice empathy and relate to the feelings of others. These activities are designed to engage children in thinking about emotions, understanding perspectives, and responding with compassion. By making empathy-building activities a regular part of a child's routine, adults can help foster empathy as a lifelong skill.

1. Emotion Charades

Emotion charades is a fun and interactive game that encourages children to identify and express emotions while also learning to recognize those emotions in others. To play, children take turns acting out different emotions—such as happiness, sadness, anger, or excitement—without using words, while the other players try to guess the emotion being portrayed. This game helps children practice reading facial expressions and body language, which are key components of empathy.

After each round, the group can discuss how they knew which emotion was being acted out and talk about what might cause someone to feel that way. This conversation reinforces emotional literacy and helps children become more aware of how emotions are expressed.

2. "Walk in Someone Else's Shoes" Activity

This activity is designed to help children practice perspective-taking by imagining what it's like to be in someone else's situation. Caregivers or teachers can present a scenario, such as, "Imagine you are the new student at school and you don't know anyone. How might you feel? What would you want others to do to help you feel welcome?" The children can then discuss or write about how they think the new student would feel and how they could offer support.

This activity can be adapted to a variety of situations, from imagining what it's like to be a younger sibling to thinking about how someone might feel after losing a pet. By encouraging children to think about the emotions of others, this activity helps build empathy and understanding.

3. Empathy in Storytelling

Storytelling provides an excellent opportunity for children to explore emotions and practice empathy. Caregivers and educators can read stories that focus on characters experiencing different emotions or challenges, and then discuss how the characters might feel and how the child might respond in a similar situation.

For example, after reading a story about a character who feels lonely, caregivers can ask questions like, "Why do you think the character felt lonely? What would you do if you saw someone feeling like that?" This type of discussion helps children practice empathy by relating to the character's emotions and considering how they might offer support.

4. Kindness Jar

A kindness jar is a simple yet effective way to encourage empathy and prosocial behavior. Children are encouraged to perform acts of kindness throughout the day—whether it's helping a friend, sharing a toy, or comforting someone who is upset. Each time a child performs an act of kindness, they write it on a small piece of paper and place it in the jar. At the end of the week or month, the group can read through the acts of kindness and celebrate the ways they helped others feel good.

This activity reinforces the idea that small acts of kindness can have a big impact on others' emotions and encourages children to look for opportunities to be empathetic and compassionate in their daily interactions. The process of reflecting on their acts of kindness also helps children recognize how their actions positively influence the emotions of those around them.

5. Empathy Role-Playing

Role-playing is a highly effective way to teach empathy by placing children in situations where they have to think about and respond to others' emotions. In this activity, children are given different scenarios to act out, such as comforting a friend who is upset, resolving a conflict with a sibling, or helping someone who is feeling nervous about a new experience.

After the role-play, children can discuss how they felt in their roles and how they chose to respond to the emotions of others. For instance, if a child was playing the role of a friend comforting someone, they can explain what they did to show empathy, such as offering a hug or using kind words. This activity allows children to practice empathetic responses in a safe and supportive environment, helping them develop the skills they need to respond to real-life emotional situations.

6. Feelings Collage

A feelings collage is an artistic activity that encourages children to explore and express different emotions through images and pictures. Children are given magazines, newspapers, or drawings and are asked to cut out images that represent various emotions, such as happiness, anger, sadness, or fear. Afterward, they glue the images onto a large piece of paper to create a collage of emotions.

Once the collage is complete, caregivers can talk with the children about the different emotions represented and discuss what might cause someone to feel that way. For example, a child might choose an image of a person smiling to represent happiness and explain that they feel happy when they play with their friends. This activity helps children make connections between visual representations of emotions and real-life experiences, fostering emotional awareness and empathy.

7. "How Would You Feel If…" Game

This game involves presenting hypothetical scenarios to children and asking them to imagine how they would feel in that situation. For example, the adult might ask, "How would you feel if someone took your favorite toy without asking?" or "How would you feel if a friend didn't invite you to their birthday party?"

After discussing their own feelings, the adult can ask the children to consider how others might feel in the same situation, encouraging them to practice perspective-taking. This game helps children develop their ability to empathize by thinking about how different situations affect both themselves and others emotionally.

8. Emotion Matching Games

Emotion matching games are another effective way to help children recognize and relate to different feelings. In this activity, children are presented with pairs of cards, with one card showing a facial expression (such as a sad or happy face) and the other card showing a scenario (such as a child dropping their ice cream or getting a hug). The goal of the game is to match the correct emotion with the appropriate scenario.

This type of game helps children practice recognizing emotional cues and linking those cues to real-life situations. It also reinforces the idea that different situations can evoke a variety of emotions, helping children understand the emotional experiences of others.

9. Gratitude Circle

Gratitude circles are group activities that encourage children to express appreciation for one another, fostering a sense of empathy and community. In a gratitude circle, children sit in a circle and take turns saying something kind or appreciative about the person next to them. For example, one child might say, "I'm thankful that you helped me with my homework," or "I appreciate how you shared your toys with me yesterday."

This activity not only promotes positive social interactions but also encourages children to think about how their actions affect the feelings of others. Expressing gratitude helps children develop empathy by recognizing the positive impact of kindness and support on their peers.

10. Empathy Journals

An empathy journal is a reflective activity that encourages children to think about the emotions and experiences of others. Each day or week, children are asked to write or draw about a time when they noticed someone feeling a particular emotion and how they responded—or could have responded—with empathy. For example, a child might write about a time when they saw a friend feeling sad because they lost a game, and how they offered to play with them afterward.

The process of reflecting on these interactions helps children become more aware of their own empathy and the ways they can support others emotionally. It also gives them a chance to think about situations where they might improve their empathetic responses in the future.

11. "What Would You Do?" Cards

This activity involves creating cards with different social scenarios that require an empathetic response. For example, one card might describe a situation where a classmate falls down and hurts themselves during recess, while another card might describe a friend feeling anxious about giving a presentation in front of the class.

Children are then asked to read the scenario and explain what they would do to help or comfort the person in the situation. This activity encourages children to think critically about how they can show empathy and respond to the emotions of others in various contexts.

12. Collaborative Art Projects

Collaborative art projects, such as group murals or shared sculptures, require children to work together to achieve a common goal. These projects foster empathy by encouraging children to consider the ideas and feelings of their peers as they collaborate on the artwork. For example, one child might want to paint a particular part of the mural, while another has a different idea. Through discussion and compromise, the children learn to navigate each other's emotions and find a solution that works for everyone.

These collaborative projects provide valuable opportunities for children to practice empathy in a hands-on way, as they learn to communicate, cooperate, and respond to each other's emotions and perspectives.

13. Empathy in Action: Community Service

Engaging children in community service activities, such as collecting food for a local shelter or helping to clean up a neighborhood park, provides real-life opportunities to practice empathy and compassion. These activities help children see firsthand the positive impact of helping others and encourage them to think about the needs and feelings of people in their community.

For example, after participating in a food drive, a caregiver might talk with the child about how their efforts will help families who might be struggling, reinforcing the importance of empathy and understanding for those in different circumstances.

14. Mirror Games

Mirror games involve two children standing face-to-face, with one acting as the "leader" and the other as the "mirror." The leader makes facial expressions that represent different emotions, such as smiling, frowning, or looking surprised, while the mirror imitates the expression exactly. After a few minutes, the roles switch, giving both children a chance to lead and mirror.

This activity helps children practice recognizing and mimicking emotional expressions, which strengthens their ability to read and understand others' emotions in real-life social situations.

15. Discussing Real-World Events

For older children, discussing real-world events, such as natural disasters, global conflicts, or social justice issues, can be an effective way to promote empathy. Caregivers and educators can share news stories or videos that highlight the experiences of people facing difficult challenges and encourage children to reflect on how those individuals might be feeling.

For example, after watching a news story about a community affected by a hurricane, a caregiver might ask, "How do you think the people who lost their homes are feeling right now? What do you think we could do to help?" These discussions help children expand their empathy beyond their immediate environment and consider the emotions and needs of people in different parts of the world.

These activities, when integrated into daily routines and interactions, can significantly strengthen a child's ability to understand and respond to the emotions of others. By practicing empathy through games, storytelling, and real-life experiences, children learn to connect more deeply with those around them, fostering a sense of compassion, understanding, and emotional intelligence. As they grow, these early lessons in empathy will continue to influence their relationships, decision-making, and contributions to their communities, setting the foundation for a lifetime of meaningful, supportive interactions.

Teaching Self-Regulation to Children

What Self-Regulation Looks Like at Different Ages

Self-regulation is the ability to manage one's emotions, behaviors, and thoughts in a way that is appropriate for the situation at hand. This crucial skill develops gradually as children grow, helping them navigate the complexities of their emotional experiences, maintain control over their actions, and make thoughtful decisions. However, the way self-regulation manifests differs significantly at various developmental stages, reflecting the cognitive, social, and emotional maturity of the child.

In infancy, self-regulation is largely dependent on external support. Newborns and young infants have very limited ability to control their emotions or behaviors. When they feel discomfort, hunger, or distress, they rely on crying as their primary means of communication and emotional release. During this time, parents and caregivers play a critical role in co-regulation, meaning they soothe the child's emotions through physical comfort, feeding, or rocking. While infants are not capable of independent self-regulation, the process of being comforted by a caregiver helps them develop the neural pathways necessary for future emotional regulation. For example, when a parent consistently responds to a crying baby with warmth and care, the child begins to associate comfort with emotional distress, laying the foundation for eventual self-soothing behaviors.

By the toddler years (ages 1 to 3), children begin to develop rudimentary self-regulation skills, though they are still highly reactive and reliant on caregivers for guidance. Toddlers experience intense emotions, often moving quickly between happiness, frustration, anger, or sadness. This is the age of tantrums, which are common when toddlers are overwhelmed by emotions they cannot yet control. For example, a toddler might throw a tantrum when they are frustrated by not getting what they want, or when they are tired but unable to express it in words. At this stage, self-regulation is largely a learning process, with toddlers experimenting with how to manage their emotions. They may start using simple strategies like sucking their thumb, holding a comfort object like a blanket, or seeking out a parent for reassurance.

As children move into early childhood (ages 3 to 5), they begin to show more advanced signs of self-regulation. Preschool-aged children have developed better language skills, which allows them to express their emotions verbally rather than through physical outbursts. For example, a preschooler might say, "I'm mad because my toy broke," instead of immediately throwing the toy in frustration. While emotional outbursts still happen, especially when children are tired or hungry, preschoolers are more capable of pausing before reacting. They may start to use simple techniques like taking deep breaths, counting to ten, or asking for help when they are upset. Social interactions with peers also play a significant role in developing self-regulation at this age. Children begin to understand the concept of waiting their turn, sharing toys, and resolving conflicts with the help of a teacher or caregiver.

In early elementary school (ages 6 to 8), self-regulation becomes more consistent, though children still require guidance in managing strong emotions. At this age, children are better able to control their impulses and delay gratification. For instance, a child might resist the urge to interrupt a conversation or wait until after finishing homework to play with their favorite toy. Emotional regulation is increasingly influenced by social norms, with children beginning to understand that certain behaviors are expected in different situations, such as being quiet during class or taking turns in a game. However, children in this age group may still struggle with frustration, especially in challenging academic or social situations. They might become upset if they can't solve a difficult math problem or if they feel excluded by peers. Caregivers and teachers play an important role in helping children navigate these moments by offering strategies for managing frustration and building resilience.

By later elementary school (ages 9 to 11), children demonstrate a much greater capacity for self-regulation. They are better able to identify their emotions, understand the reasons behind them, and choose appropriate responses. For example, a child in this age group might recognize that they are feeling anxious before a test and use coping strategies like reviewing their notes or practicing deep breathing to calm down. Social awareness also grows during this time, with children becoming more attuned to how their emotions and behaviors affect others. They are more likely to manage their impulses in social situations, such as controlling their temper during a disagreement with a friend or teacher. However, emotional regulation can still be a challenge, particularly in situations that trigger strong feelings of anger, disappointment, or embarrassment. Children may need reminders and guidance from adults to apply their self-regulation strategies consistently.

In early adolescence (ages 12 to 14), self-regulation becomes more complex due to the physical and emotional changes associated with puberty. Adolescents experience heightened emotional intensity, often feeling overwhelmed by emotions like frustration, anger, or anxiety. At this stage, self-regulation is not only about managing impulses but also about navigating the deeper emotional experiences that come with growing independence, identity formation, and peer relationships. For instance, an adolescent might need to regulate their emotions during a disagreement with a parent or friend, choosing to stay calm instead of lashing out. However, this is also a time when impulsivity can peak, leading to emotional outbursts, risk-taking behaviors, or conflicts with authority figures. Adolescents benefit from having adults in their lives who provide both emotional support and structure, helping them develop stronger self-regulation skills.

By late adolescence (ages 15 to 18), self-regulation becomes more mature and reflective. Adolescents are more capable of pausing to reflect on their emotional responses before acting. For example, they might take time to cool down after an argument with a peer instead of immediately responding in anger. Self-regulation at this stage involves not only managing emotions but also setting long-term goals and maintaining focus in the face of distractions or challenges. Adolescents develop a deeper understanding of the consequences of their actions and are better able to delay gratification in pursuit of larger goals, such as studying for exams or saving money for a desired purchase. However, emotional regulation can still be difficult in high-stress situations, such as facing academic pressure or navigating romantic relationships. Adolescents continue to refine their self-regulation skills through experience and feedback from trusted adults.

Throughout childhood and adolescence, self-regulation is a dynamic skill that evolves with age, experience, and cognitive development. While younger children rely heavily on caregivers to help them manage their emotions, older children and adolescents gradually take on more responsibility for their own emotional regulation. Caregivers and educators play a critical role in supporting this development by providing guidance, modeling self-regulation, and creating environments where children can practice these skills.

Techniques to Help Children Calm Down and Reflect

Helping children develop effective self-regulation techniques is essential for their emotional well-being and success in social and academic settings. There are several strategies that caregivers and educators can use to teach children how to calm down and reflect on their emotions, which in turn helps them manage their behaviors in a constructive way.

One of the most fundamental techniques for self-regulation is deep breathing. Deep breathing helps calm the body's stress response by activating the parasympathetic nervous system, which counteracts the fight-or-flight reaction triggered by strong emotions. Teaching children to take slow, deep breaths when they are feeling overwhelmed or upset can help them regain control of their emotions and think more clearly. For example, a child who is frustrated during a difficult homework assignment might be encouraged to stop, close their eyes, and take a few deep breaths before continuing. Deep breathing is simple to teach and can be practiced anywhere, making it a versatile tool for emotional regulation.

Another useful technique is mindfulness, which involves paying attention to the present moment without judgment. Mindfulness helps children become more aware of their thoughts and emotions, allowing them to recognize when they are becoming upset or overwhelmed before their emotions escalate. For example, a child who is feeling anxious about a school project might practice mindfulness by focusing on their breathing or by noticing the sensations in their body, such as tension in their shoulders or a rapid heartbeat. By acknowledging these physical and emotional cues, the child can take steps to calm down before their anxiety takes over. Mindfulness exercises, such as guided meditations or body scans, can be incorporated into a child's daily routine to help them build emotional awareness and self-regulation skills.

Visualization is another powerful tool for helping children calm down and reflect on their emotions. Visualization involves imagining a peaceful or positive scene, such as being at the beach, lying in a sunny field, or playing with a beloved pet. This mental imagery can help children shift their focus away from stressful or upsetting thoughts and toward a more calming, positive experience. For example, if a child is feeling nervous before a big event, they might close their eyes and imagine themselves in a place where they feel safe and happy. Visualization can also be used as part of a bedtime routine to help children wind down and relax before going to sleep.

Progressive muscle relaxation is another technique that can help children calm down by reducing physical tension. This method involves tensing and then relaxing different muscle groups in the body, helping children release physical stress and focus their attention on the process of relaxation. For example, a child might be guided to tense their hands into fists for a few seconds, then slowly release the tension, noticing how their hands feel afterward. This technique can be especially helpful for children who tend to hold tension in their bodies when they are stressed or anxious.

In addition to these physical relaxation techniques, emotion labeling is an important strategy for helping children reflect on their feelings. When children are able to name their emotions, they gain a better understanding of what they are experiencing and why. For instance, if a child is feeling frustrated because they are struggling with a task, a caregiver might say, "It seems like you're feeling really frustrated because the puzzle pieces aren't fitting together. Let's take a break and figure out what's making it difficult." By naming the emotion and acknowledging the child's struggle, caregivers help the child feel understood, which can reduce the intensity of the emotion. This technique not only validates the child's experience but also gives them the vocabulary to describe their emotions in the future, which is a key component of self-regulation.

Using a feelings chart can be another helpful tool for emotion labeling, particularly for younger children who may struggle to articulate their feelings verbally. A feelings chart typically displays a range of facial expressions representing different emotions, such as happy, sad, angry, frustrated, or excited. When children are feeling overwhelmed, caregivers can encourage them to point to the face that best represents their current emotion. This activity helps children identify their emotions more easily and serves as a visual reminder that all emotions are normal and manageable.

Another effective strategy for promoting self-regulation is teaching children to engage in positive self-talk. Positive self-talk involves encouraging oneself with kind, supportive statements rather than focusing on negative or self-critical thoughts. For instance, if a child is feeling discouraged after making a mistake, they might be taught to say, "It's okay to make mistakes. I can try again," rather than thinking, "I'm no good at this." Caregivers can model positive self-talk by using encouraging language in difficult situations. For example, a parent might say, "I know this is tough, but I'm proud of you for trying, and I know you can figure it out." By practicing positive self-talk, children learn to challenge negative thinking and maintain a more balanced emotional response to challenges.

Taking a break is another valuable self-regulation technique, particularly for children who are feeling overwhelmed by strong emotions. When emotions like frustration, anger, or sadness start to escalate, taking a short break from the situation can give the child time to calm down and gain perspective. For example, if a child is feeling upset during a disagreement with a sibling, they might be encouraged to step away for a few minutes to cool down before re-engaging in the conversation. During the break, the child can practice deep breathing, visualization, or another calming technique to help them reset emotionally. Afterward, they can return to the situation with a clearer mind and a more balanced emotional state. Teaching children to recognize when they need a break and to take one before emotions escalate is a crucial part of developing self-regulation.

Using physical activity as a way to release emotional energy is another important strategy, especially for children who have difficulty sitting still or who tend to express their emotions physically. Engaging in physical activities like running, jumping, dancing, or even doing simple exercises like stretching can help children release built-up tension and return to a calmer state. For example, a child who is feeling angry after a conflict might be encouraged to run around in the yard for a few minutes to let off steam before discussing their feelings. Physical activity not only helps to regulate emotions by reducing stress but also gives children a constructive outlet for managing their emotional energy.

Teaching problem-solving skills is also essential for helping children manage their emotions in challenging situations. When children are faced with a problem that triggers an emotional response, such as a disagreement with a friend or a difficult school assignment, they may feel overwhelmed if they don't know how to handle the situation. By guiding children through the problem-solving process, caregivers can help them break down the situation into manageable steps. For example, if a child is upset because a friend didn't want to play with them, a caregiver might help them brainstorm possible solutions, such as asking the friend why they didn't want to play, finding a different activity, or asking someone else to join them. This process helps the child regain a sense of control over the situation, reducing feelings of helplessness and frustration.

Creating a calm-down corner in the home or classroom can also support self-regulation by providing children with a designated space to relax and reflect when they are feeling overwhelmed. A calm-down corner might include items like soft pillows, calming visuals, sensory toys, or a small tent where the child can retreat when they need a break. This space gives children a safe, comfortable place to process their emotions in private, away from the source of stress. Encouraging children to use the calm-down corner when they feel their emotions escalating teaches them that it's okay to take time to calm down before addressing a problem.

Routine and structure are also important elements in fostering self-regulation, particularly for younger children. Predictable routines help children feel secure and in control, which can reduce anxiety and emotional outbursts. When children know what to expect during the day—such as set times for meals, play, and rest—they are better able to manage transitions and cope with unexpected challenges. For example, a child who knows that they have a scheduled time for free play after finishing their homework is more likely to stay focused on their task, knowing that a reward is coming. Clear expectations and consistent routines provide a framework that supports self-regulation by reducing uncertainty and helping children anticipate what comes next.

Modeling self-regulation is perhaps one of the most powerful ways caregivers can teach this skill to children. Children learn by observing the behaviors of the adults around them, so when caregivers model healthy emotional regulation, children are more likely to adopt similar strategies. For instance, if a parent or teacher is feeling frustrated by a challenging situation, they might verbalize their self-regulation process by saying, "I'm feeling a little frustrated right now, so I'm going to take a deep breath and think about how to handle this." By seeing adults manage their emotions in a calm, thoughtful way, children learn that they too can manage their emotions constructively.

Another strategy is practicing reflection with children after an emotional incident. Once the child has calmed down, caregivers can help them reflect on what happened and how they responded to their emotions. This process of reflection allows children to think critically about their emotional responses and consider alternative ways of handling similar situations in the future. For example, after a child has calmed down from a tantrum, a caregiver might say, "What do you think made you feel so upset? Next time, what could you do to calm down before you get too frustrated?" This type of reflective conversation helps children develop greater self-awareness and reinforces the self-regulation strategies they are learning.

Incorporating emotional vocabulary into these reflective conversations is also key. When caregivers help children label their emotions during reflection, they build the child's ability to recognize and manage those emotions in the future. For example, after a child has thrown a tantrum because they were told they couldn't have a snack before dinner, a caregiver might say, "It seems like you were feeling disappointed and maybe a little angry when you couldn't have a snack. It's okay to feel that way, but next time, let's try taking some deep breaths when we feel angry." This approach not only validates the child's feelings but also helps them understand how to use self-regulation strategies in the future.

Self-regulation is a skill that requires time, patience, and consistent practice. By teaching children techniques like deep breathing, mindfulness, positive self-talk, and problem-solving, caregivers and educators provide them with a toolkit for managing their emotions and behaviors in a healthy way. As children grow, these techniques become an integral part of their emotional regulation process, helping them navigate the challenges of daily life with greater resilience and confidence. Through thoughtful guidance and support, children can learn to manage their emotions, reflect on their experiences, and develop the self-regulation skills that will serve them Throughout their lives.

Problem-Solving Skills for Emotional Situations

E ncouraging Critical Thinking in Emotional Conflicts

Developing problem-solving skills is essential for children as they encounter emotional conflicts throughout their lives. These skills not only help children navigate their feelings but also enable them to address interpersonal challenges and manage stress more effectively. By teaching children to approach emotional situations with a problem-solving mindset, caregivers and educators can empower them to think critically, assess their emotions, and respond constructively.

Encouraging critical thinking in emotional conflicts requires helping children understand that emotions and conflicts are natural and can be addressed thoughtfully rather than reactively. Often, children experience intense emotions—such as frustration, anger, or sadness—that can cloud their judgment, leading to impulsive or defensive behaviors. By encouraging children to pause and think critically, they can begin to assess the situation from different angles and make decisions that are both emotionally intelligent and effective.

One of the foundational steps in fostering critical thinking during emotional conflicts is teaching children how to identify the problem clearly. Many emotional conflicts arise when children feel misunderstood, frustrated, or unfairly treated, but they may not fully grasp what is causing their distress. By guiding children to articulate the root of their problem, they can begin to disentangle their emotions from the conflict itself. For example, if a child is upset because they didn't get picked for a game at recess, they might initially express their frustration through anger, saying something like, "Nobody likes me!" A caregiver or teacher can help them critically assess the situation by asking, "What exactly made you feel upset?" This prompts the child to reflect and recognize that it wasn't personal rejection but perhaps a misunderstanding or a missed opportunity that triggered their emotions.

Once the problem is identified, it's important to teach children to analyze their emotions. Emotional awareness is a key aspect of critical thinking in emotional situations. Children need to be able to distinguish between different emotions and understand how these feelings might influence their responses. For example, in a conflict with a peer, a child might feel a mix of emotions, such as anger, jealousy, or sadness. Teaching the child to reflect on these emotions—by asking questions like "Are you angry because you felt left out?" or "Do you think you're frustrated because you wanted to do better in the game?"—helps them gain clarity on the situation and reduces the likelihood of reactive, emotionally charged responses.

Perspective-taking is another essential component of critical thinking during emotional conflicts. Teaching children to consider the perspectives of others involved in the conflict can help them develop empathy and find solutions that benefit everyone. For instance, if two children are arguing over a toy, a caregiver might encourage each child to explain how they feel about the situation and why they want the toy. This approach allows both children to hear each other's perspectives, making it easier for them to find a compromise. Additionally, perspective-taking helps children understand that conflicts often arise from misunderstandings or differing needs, rather than intentional harm. By learning to put themselves in someone else's shoes, children can approach conflicts with more compassion and a greater willingness to collaborate on a solution.

Evaluating options is a critical thinking skill that children can apply to problem-solving in emotional conflicts. Once the child has identified the problem and reflected on their emotions, they need to consider different ways to resolve the situation. Caregivers can encourage children to brainstorm a variety of possible solutions, even if some of those ideas seem far-fetched or unrealistic. For example, if a child is upset because they didn't get their way in a group activity, the caregiver might ask, "What are some things you could do to make the situation better?" The child might come up with ideas like "I could ask to play a different game" or "I could take turns with my friends." This brainstorming process encourages children to think creatively and assess which options are most likely to lead to a positive outcome.

When evaluating solutions, it's also important for children to consider the consequences of each option. Caregivers can guide children through this process by asking questions like, "What do you think will happen if you choose this option?" or "How might your friend feel if you do that?" By thinking about the potential outcomes of their actions, children learn to weigh the pros and cons of different approaches and make more informed decisions. For example, if a child is considering walking away from a friend who hurt their feelings, they might realize that while it would make them feel better in the short term, it could damage the friendship in the long run. Encouraging children to reflect on the consequences of their actions helps them develop emotional foresight and make choices that align with their values and long-term goals.

In addition to evaluating solutions, children also need to learn how to implement and review their decisions. After choosing a solution, it's important for children to follow through and assess whether their approach was successful. For example, if a child decides to resolve a conflict with a friend by apologizing, they can reflect afterward on how the friend responded and whether the situation improved. If the solution didn't work as expected, caregivers can help the child reflect on what they might do differently next time. This review process reinforces critical thinking by teaching children that problem-solving is an ongoing, iterative process, and that it's okay to try different approaches until they find one that works.

Encouraging critical thinking in emotional conflicts helps children build confidence in their ability to navigate challenging situations. When children know that they have the tools to think through problems and come up with solutions, they feel more empowered and less overwhelmed by their emotions. This sense of agency not only improves their emotional well-being but also strengthens their relationships and social interactions.

Role-playing Scenarios to Practice Problem-Solving

Role-playing is an excellent tool for helping children practice problem-solving in emotional situations. By acting out different scenarios, children have the opportunity to explore various ways of handling conflicts, expressing emotions, and finding solutions, all in a safe and supportive environment. Role-playing allows children to practice the problem-solving skills they are learning, such as identifying problems, reflecting on emotions, considering others' perspectives, and evaluating solutions, without the pressure of real-life consequences.

Scenario 1: Conflict Over Sharing a Toy

In this scenario, two children are arguing over a toy that both want to play with. The caregiver can guide the role-play by asking one child to pretend they are upset because they didn't get the toy, while the other child explains why they want it. Through this role-playing exercise, the children can practice identifying the problem (both want the same toy), reflecting on their emotions (one child feels frustrated, while the other feels disappointed), and considering solutions (taking turns, playing together, or finding another toy).

After acting out the scenario, the caregiver can lead a discussion about the different solutions and their potential outcomes. For example, "What do you think would happen if you shared the toy?" or "How would you feel if your friend let you play with it first?" This reflective conversation helps children understand the importance of compromise and empathy in resolving conflicts.

Scenario 2: Dealing with Exclusion in a Group Activity

In this role-play, one child feels excluded from a group activity at recess and is upset that their friends didn't include them. The child can practice expressing their feelings by saying something like, "I felt really sad when you didn't let me join the game." The other children in the role-play can respond by explaining why they made that decision, and the group can work together to find a solution that includes everyone. Possible solutions might include inviting the excluded child to join the game next time or finding a new activity that everyone can enjoy together.

Role-playing this scenario allows children to practice perspective-taking by understanding how exclusion can affect someone's emotions. It also teaches them how to express their feelings in a calm and constructive way, rather than resorting to anger or withdrawal.

Scenario 3: Resolving a Misunderstanding Between Friends

In this scenario, two children have had a misunderstanding that led to hurt feelings. For example, one child may have accidentally taken something that belonged to the other, leading to an argument. Through role-play, the children can practice explaining their perspectives and working toward a resolution. One child might say, "I didn't realize that was your pencil. I thought it was mine," while the other child can express how they felt when their pencil was taken.

The role-play encourages the children to reflect on the misunderstanding and consider solutions such as apologizing, returning the item, or offering to share. After the role-play, the caregiver can guide a discussion about how misunderstandings happen and how important communication is in preventing and resolving conflicts.

Scenario 4: Handling Frustration with a Difficult Task

This role-play focuses on helping a child manage frustration during a challenging task, such as a difficult homework assignment. The child can act out feeling frustrated, saying something like, "I can't do this! It's too hard!" The caregiver or teacher in the role-play can guide the child through problem-solving by helping them identify the source of their frustration and suggesting strategies for calming down and tackling the task one step at a time.

For example, the caregiver might encourage the child to take a short break, use positive self-talk ("I can try again, and I'll get better with practice"), or ask for help. This role-play helps the child practice using self-regulation and critical thinking to solve a problem, rather than giving up in frustration.

Scenario 5: Navigating Peer Pressure

In this scenario, a child faces peer pressure from friends who are encouraging them to do something they feel uncomfortable with, such as breaking a rule or excluding another classmate. The role-play allows the child to practice standing up for themselves and expressing their feelings about the situation. For example, the child might say, "I don't think it's fair to leave them out. I want to include everyone."

This role-playing scenario helps children practice assertiveness and problem-solving in a peer context, teaching them how to navigate peer pressure while staying true to their values. After the role-play, the caregiver can lead a discussion on why it's important to express one's feelings honestly, even when facing peer pressure, and how finding a solution that respects everyone's needs is a positive approach to conflict resolution.

Scenario 6: Coping with Jealousy Between Siblings

Sibling rivalry often involves feelings of jealousy, which can lead to arguments or emotional conflicts. In this role-play scenario, one child might express jealousy because they feel their sibling is getting more attention or has better toys. The caregiver can guide the children through a role-play where the jealous sibling shares their feelings ("I feel upset because you got a new toy, and I didn't"), while the other sibling can respond with empathy.

This role-play helps children practice articulating their feelings instead of acting out through conflict. The discussion afterward can focus on recognizing and managing jealousy in healthy ways, such as talking openly with parents, finding ways to share, or focusing on the positive aspects of their relationship with their sibling. The goal is for children to understand that jealousy is a normal emotion and that expressing it calmly can help solve problems.

Scenario 7: Responding to Criticism or Negative Feedback

Children often struggle with handling criticism or negative feedback, which can lead to defensiveness or feelings of inadequacy. In this role-play scenario, a child might act out a situation where they received criticism about their schoolwork or behavior. For example, a teacher might say, "You didn't follow the instructions on this assignment," and the child can practice how to respond constructively.

Through role-playing, the child can practice self-regulation by acknowledging the feedback without becoming defensive. For example, they might say, "I didn't realize I made that mistake. I'll try to fix it." This exercise teaches children how to manage the emotional discomfort that often accompanies criticism and how to respond with a problem-solving mindset rather than reacting emotionally.

Scenario 8: Handling Disappointment When Things Don't Go as Planned

In this role-play scenario, a child might express disappointment when something doesn't go as expected—such as a canceled play date, losing a game, or not being chosen for a team. The child can act out their initial reaction, such as feeling sad or frustrated, and then practice finding ways to cope with the disappointment.

For example, the caregiver might encourage the child to reflect on their feelings by saying, "It's okay to feel disappointed, but what could you do to make yourself feel better?" This role-play teaches children that while they can't always control external events, they can control how they respond to them. The discussion afterward can focus on developing strategies for handling disappointment, such as finding alternative activities, practicing gratitude, or seeking comfort from a trusted adult.

Scenario 9: Mediating a Conflict Between Friends

In this scenario, a child might act as a mediator between two friends who are having a disagreement. This role-playing exercise encourages the mediator to listen to both sides of the conflict, understand each person's perspective, and suggest possible solutions.

For example, if two friends are arguing over who gets to choose the next game, the mediator might say, "I understand that you both want to choose. What if we take turns picking games?" This role-play helps children practice active listening, empathy, and collaborative problem-solving. It also reinforces the idea that conflicts can often be resolved peacefully when everyone's perspective is considered.

Scenario 10: Handling Bullying or Unkind Behavior

In this role-play, a child can practice responding to bullying or unkind behavior from a peer. The child might act out a situation where someone said something hurtful to them, and they have to decide how to respond. The caregiver can guide the child in considering options such as standing up for themselves calmly, seeking help from a trusted adult, or walking away from the situation.

This role-play teaches children that they have multiple options for handling difficult social situations and that responding assertively, rather than aggressively or passively, is often the best approach. The follow-up discussion can emphasize the importance of maintaining self-respect and seeking support when dealing with unkind behavior.

Scenario 11: Apologizing After a Mistake

Apologizing is a critical part of resolving conflicts and maintaining healthy relationships. In this role-play, a child can practice apologizing after making a mistake, such as accidentally hurting a friend's feelings or breaking a sibling's toy. The child might say, "I'm sorry for what I did. I didn't mean to hurt your feelings," and the other person can practice accepting the apology and discussing how to move forward.

This role-play helps children understand that making mistakes is a normal part of life and that apologizing is a constructive way to repair relationships. The caregiver can lead a discussion on how sincere apologies can help both parties feel better and how it's important to learn from mistakes rather than feeling ashamed of them.

Scenario 12: Handling Fairness Issues in Group Activities

Fairness is often a source of conflict in group activities, especially when children feel that rules aren't being followed or that someone is getting special treatment. In this role-play, a child might express frustration that they weren't given a fair chance to participate in a game or activity. The caregiver can guide the children in discussing their perspectives and coming up with a fair solution, such as creating clear rules or taking turns.

This role-play teaches children to address fairness issues calmly and to find solutions that ensure everyone feels included and respected. It also emphasizes the importance of setting clear expectations in group activities to prevent conflicts.

Scenario 13: Managing Anxiety in New Situations

In this scenario, a child might act out a situation where they are feeling anxious about a new experience, such as starting a new school, joining a new team, or giving a presentation in front of the class. The role-play allows the child to express their anxiety ("I'm really nervous about meeting new people") and practice coping strategies, such as deep breathing, visualization, or positive self-talk.

After the role-play, the caregiver can guide a discussion on how anxiety is a normal response to new situations and how practicing self-regulation techniques can help them manage their emotions. This role-play helps children build resilience by showing them that they can face new challenges and succeed.

By engaging in these role-playing scenarios, children not only learn problem-solving skills but also practice empathy, emotional regulation, and communication. Each scenario provides a safe space for children to explore different ways of handling emotional conflicts and to reflect on the outcomes of their decisions. Over time, these role-playing exercises help children internalize problem-solving strategies, making them better equipped to navigate real-life emotional situations with confidence and resilience.

Mindfulness and Emotional Control

The Benefits of Mindfulness in Emotional Regulation

Mindfulness is a powerful tool that can greatly aid children in developing emotional regulation skills. Emotional regulation refers to the ability to manage and respond to emotional experiences in a healthy and controlled manner. For children, who often experience intense emotions such as frustration, anger, excitement, and sadness, learning how to regulate these feelings is essential for their emotional development and well-being. Mindfulness is an effective method for helping children achieve this by teaching them to focus on the present moment, recognize their emotional state, and respond thoughtfully rather than reactively.

At its core, mindfulness involves paying attention to the present moment without judgment. For children, this practice allows them to become more aware of their thoughts, emotions, and bodily sensations. Often, children may react impulsively to their emotions because they do not have the self-awareness to recognize what they are feeling in the moment. This can lead to emotional outbursts or actions that they later regret, such as lashing out at a peer in anger or crying out of frustration. Mindfulness helps children slow down, tune into their emotions, and make conscious choices about how to respond, rather than letting their emotions control their behavior.

One of the primary benefits of mindfulness in emotional regulation is that it promotes self-awareness. When children practice mindfulness, they become more attuned to their internal emotional states and can more easily recognize when they are beginning to feel angry, sad, or anxious. This self-awareness is the first step toward emotional regulation, as it allows children to identify their feelings before they escalate into uncontrollable reactions. For example, a child who has learned mindfulness techniques might notice that they are starting to feel frustrated during a difficult homework assignment. Instead of immediately reacting by throwing their pencil in frustration, the child can take a mindful pause, acknowledge their frustration, and decide to take a short break or ask for help.

Mindfulness also teaches children self-acceptance, which is crucial for emotional control. Children often struggle with negative emotions, such as anger or jealousy, because they feel these emotions are bad or wrong. This judgment can create internal conflict, leading children to suppress or deny their feelings, which can make emotional regulation more difficult. Mindfulness encourages children to accept their emotions without judgment, recognizing that all emotions—whether positive or negative—are a natural part of life. By accepting their feelings as they arise, children are less likely to be overwhelmed by them and can focus on managing their emotions in healthy ways. For example, a child practicing mindfulness might say to themselves, "I'm feeling really angry right now, and that's okay. I can take a few deep breaths to calm down." This acceptance helps the child regulate their emotions rather than fighting against them.

Another significant benefit of mindfulness is its ability to reduce stress and anxiety in children. Many children experience stress and anxiety, whether due to academic pressures, social dynamics, or other challenges. When left unchecked, these emotions can lead to emotional outbursts, difficulty concentrating, and even physical symptoms such as headaches or stomachaches. Mindfulness helps children manage stress by teaching them to stay grounded in the present moment rather than becoming overwhelmed by future worries or past regrets. For example, a child who feels anxious about an upcoming test might practice mindfulness by focusing on their breathing and reminding themselves that they are prepared for the test and can handle whatever comes. This focus on the present helps reduce the intensity of their anxiety and allows them to approach the test with a clearer, calmer mind.

Mindfulness also enhances emotional resilience in children, meaning they are better able to bounce back from setbacks and challenges. Emotional resilience is the ability to recover from difficult emotions, such as sadness, disappointment, or frustration, without becoming stuck in those feelings. When children practice mindfulness, they learn that emotions are temporary and that they have the ability to manage them. For instance, a child who feels disappointed after losing a game might practice mindfulness by acknowledging their disappointment, taking a few deep breaths, and then shifting their focus to how they can improve for next time. This ability to move through difficult emotions without being overwhelmed by them is a key aspect of emotional regulation and resilience.

In addition to these emotional benefits, mindfulness also improves attention and focus, which are closely linked to emotional regulation. When children are distracted or unable to concentrate, they are more likely to become frustrated or overwhelmed by their emotions. Mindfulness teaches children to direct their attention to the task at hand, which not only helps them perform better academically but also allows them to stay calm and focused in emotionally charged situations. For example, if a child is struggling to complete a challenging math problem, mindfulness can help them focus on the steps they need to take rather than becoming frustrated by the overall difficulty of the task. This ability to focus on the present moment reduces the likelihood of emotional outbursts and helps children approach challenges with a calm and focused mindset.

Mindfulness also fosters empathy and compassion, both of which are important for emotional regulation, especially in social situations. Children who practice mindfulness are more likely to recognize and understand the emotions of others, which helps them respond with kindness and patience rather than reacting impulsively. For example, a child who sees a friend feeling upset might practice mindfulness by pausing to consider how their friend is feeling and offering comfort or support rather than ignoring or becoming impatient with them. This empathy allows children to navigate social interactions with greater emotional awareness, leading to more positive and harmonious relationships.

Overall, mindfulness is a powerful tool for helping children develop emotional regulation skills. By promoting self-awareness, self-acceptance, and emotional resilience, mindfulness helps children manage their emotions in a healthy and controlled way. These skills not only benefit children in the short term, by reducing emotional outbursts and improving focus, but also set the foundation for long-term emotional well-being.

Fun and Easy Mindfulness Exercises for Kids

Teaching mindfulness to children doesn't have to be complicated or time-consuming. There are many fun and easy exercises that can introduce mindfulness in a way that is engaging and accessible for kids. These exercises help children develop self-awareness, focus, and emotional regulation, all while having fun.

1. Belly Breathing (or Balloon Breathing)

Belly breathing is a simple mindfulness exercise that helps children focus on their breath and calm their bodies. To practice belly breathing, ask the child to lie down on their back and place their hands or a small stuffed animal on their stomach. Encourage them to take slow, deep breaths in through their nose, filling their belly like a balloon, and then slowly exhale through their mouth, letting the balloon deflate. As they breathe in and out, they can watch their stomach rise and fall, focusing on the movement.

This exercise is particularly helpful for calming down when a child is feeling anxious, frustrated, or upset. Belly breathing helps activate the body's relaxation response, slowing the heart rate and promoting a sense of calm. It's also a great tool for teaching children how to tune into their bodies and recognize when they need to take a moment to breathe and reset.

2. Mindful Listening

Mindful listening is a fun exercise that encourages children to focus on the sounds around them, helping them develop concentration and awareness of their environment. To practice mindful listening, ask the child to sit quietly and close their eyes. Then, have them listen closely to the sounds around them for one or two minutes. These sounds might include birds chirping, cars passing by, people talking, or even the sound of their own breathing. After the time is up, ask the child to describe what they heard.

This exercise teaches children to focus their attention on the present moment and helps them develop the ability to concentrate on one sense at a time. It can also be a calming activity, as focusing on soothing or neutral sounds can help distract from stressful thoughts or emotions.

3. The "Five Senses" Exercise

The "Five Senses" exercise is a simple mindfulness practice that helps children ground themselves in the present moment by focusing on their sensory experiences. To do this exercise, ask the child to take a few deep breaths and then name:
   - Five things they can see
   - Four things they can hear
   - Three things they can feel
   - Two things they can smell
   - One thing they can taste (or imagine the taste of something they like)

This exercise encourages children to engage all of their senses, which helps them shift their focus away from racing thoughts or overwhelming emotions. It's especially useful for children who are feeling anxious or overstimulated, as it helps them reconnect with the present moment and regain a sense of control.

4. Body Scan

A body scan is a mindfulness exercise that teaches children to become more aware of the sensations in their bodies, which can help them manage physical and emotional tension. To guide a body scan, ask the child to lie down comfortably and close their eyes. Starting at their toes, have them focus their attention on each part of their body, noticing any sensations or tension they might feel. Slowly guide them through their feet, legs, stomach, chest, arms, hands, neck, and head, encouraging them to relax each part of their body as they go.

This exercise helps children become more attuned to the physical sensations that accompany their emotions. For example, they might notice tightness in their shoulders when they're feeling stressed or a fluttery feeling in their stomach when they're anxious. By recognizing these sensations, children can learn to release tension and calm their bodies, which in turn helps them manage their emotions more effectively.

5. Glitter Jar

A glitter jar is a simple and fun mindfulness tool that can help children visualize their emotions and practice calming down. To make a glitter jar, fill a small jar or bottle with water, add a few spoonfuls of glitter, and secure the lid tightly. When the child is feeling upset or overwhelmed, shake the jar and watch as the glitter swirls around. As the glitter settles, encourage the child to take deep breaths and imagine their thoughts and emotions settling along with the glitter.

The glitter jar serves as a visual metaphor for the mind in a state of emotional turmoil. When the glitter is swirling around, it represents how emotions can feel chaotic and overwhelming. But as the glitter slowly settles to the bottom, it mirrors the calming of the mind when we practice mindfulness. Watching the glitter settle can be very soothing for children and helps them understand that emotions, like the glitter, eventually settle if they take time to breathe and pause. This exercise is particularly effective for young children who may struggle with verbalizing their emotions.

6. Mindful Coloring

Mindful coloring is a relaxing activity that combines creativity with mindfulness. Give the child a simple coloring page or blank piece of paper and ask them to color slowly and carefully, paying close attention to the colors they choose, the way the crayon or marker feels in their hand, and the shapes they are creating. The goal is not to finish the picture quickly, but to focus fully on the process of coloring.

This activity helps children concentrate on one task at a time, which can be especially helpful when they are feeling distracted, anxious, or overwhelmed. The repetitive, calming nature of coloring helps children relax and focus on the present moment, making it an enjoyable way to practice mindfulness without the need for formal meditation.

7. "Spidey-Senses" Activity

Inspired by Spider-Man's heightened awareness of his surroundings, the "Spidey-Senses" activity encourages children to use their own senses like superheroes. Ask the child to pretend they are Spider-Man and need to be extra aware of everything happening around them. For one or two minutes, they should pay close attention to the sights, sounds, smells, and even the feel of the air around them, as though they were tuning into their "Spidey-senses."

This playful exercise is a fun way to teach children mindfulness by encouraging them to focus on their sensory experiences. It's a great way to make mindfulness feel exciting and accessible for younger children, while still helping them develop awareness and concentration.

8. Breathing Buddies

Breathing buddies is a simple yet effective mindfulness exercise that helps children focus on their breath. To do this exercise, give the child a small stuffed animal (their "breathing buddy") and ask them to lie down on their back with the buddy resting on their belly. Then, encourage the child to take slow, deep breaths in and out, watching how their breathing buddy rises and falls with each breath.

This exercise helps children practice deep, mindful breathing in a way that is engaging and interactive. The visual feedback of the stuffed animal moving up and down helps children focus on their breathing and develop greater awareness of how deep breathing can calm their body and mind.

9. Mindful Walking

Mindful walking is a great way to incorporate mindfulness into everyday activities. To practice mindful walking, take the child on a short walk, either indoors or outdoors, and encourage them to walk slowly and deliberately, paying attention to each step they take. Ask them to notice how their feet feel when they touch the ground, how their body moves as they walk, and the sounds and sights around them.

This activity helps children practice being present in the moment while engaging in a simple, repetitive task. It's a great way to introduce mindfulness to active children who may find it difficult to sit still for more traditional mindfulness exercises. Mindful walking can also be used as a calming activity when a child is feeling restless or needs a break from more structured tasks.

10. Mindful Eating

Mindful eating is a fun and engaging way to teach children about mindfulness through a sensory experience. To practice mindful eating, give the child a small piece of food, such as a raisin, a piece of fruit, or a cracker. Ask them to examine the food carefully, noticing its color, shape, and texture. Then, have them smell the food and notice how it feels in their hand before they take a small bite. Encourage them to chew slowly, paying attention to the taste and texture of the food in their mouth.

This exercise teaches children to focus on the present moment and engage their senses fully in the experience of eating. It can also help them develop a greater appreciation for the food they eat and become more aware of their body's hunger and fullness cues.

11. Thought Clouds

The Thought Clouds exercise is a mindfulness activity that helps children become more aware of their thoughts without getting caught up in them. To do this exercise, ask the child to imagine that their thoughts are like clouds in the sky. As they sit quietly and notice their thoughts, encourage them to picture each thought as a cloud that floats by. Some clouds might be big and dark, while others are small and light. The key is to observe the clouds without trying to change them or hold onto them—just let them float by.

This exercise teaches children to recognize that thoughts, like clouds, come and go. It helps them practice letting go of troubling thoughts rather than getting stuck on them, which is an important skill for managing anxiety and intrusive thoughts.

12. "Teddy Bear Tummy Ride"

This exercise is another variation of deep breathing for young children, using their favorite teddy bear or stuffed animal to help them focus on their breath. Ask the child to lie down on their back and place the teddy bear on their tummy. Tell them to watch the teddy bear rise and fall as they breathe in and out, imagining that the teddy bear is taking a gentle ride on their tummy. As they focus on the teddy bear's movements, they can also count their breaths to help them stay focused.

This exercise is particularly useful for bedtime or moments when a child needs to relax and wind down. It combines deep breathing with a playful element, making mindfulness more accessible and enjoyable for young children.

13. Mindful Art

Mindful art is an activity where children can express their creativity while practicing mindfulness. Instead of focusing on creating a finished product, children are encouraged to focus on the process of drawing or painting. They might be asked to pay attention to the feel of the crayon or brush in their hand, the texture of the paper, or the way the colors mix together.

Mindful art allows children to express themselves freely without judgment, helping them develop a non-judgmental attitude toward their own thoughts and feelings. It's also a calming and meditative activity that can help children feel more relaxed and centered.

14. Mindful Stretching or Yoga

Mindful stretching or yoga combines physical movement with mindfulness, helping children develop both body awareness and emotional regulation skills. Simple yoga poses like "tree pose," "cat-cow," or "downward dog" can be practiced slowly and mindfully, with an emphasis on how the body feels in each position. Children can be encouraged to focus on their breathing as they move from one pose to the next, noticing how their body feels and how their breath flows.

Mindful stretching or yoga helps children release physical tension, improve concentration, and stay grounded in the present moment. It's an excellent way to incorporate mindfulness into physical activity, especially for children who enjoy movement.

15. Gratitude Practice

Gratitude practice is a mindfulness exercise that helps children focus on the positive aspects of their lives. To practice gratitude, ask the child to take a few moments each day to think of three things they are grateful for. These could be anything from their family and friends to a favorite toy or a fun experience they had that day. Encourage them to reflect on how these things make them feel and why they are thankful for them.

Gratitude practice helps children develop a positive mindset and an appreciation for the good things in their lives. It also encourages them to focus on the present moment and the things they can be grateful for right now, which can improve their overall sense of well-being.

These fun and easy mindfulness exercises offer children engaging ways to practice emotional regulation and develop greater self-awareness. By incorporating mindfulness into their daily routines, children can learn to manage their emotions more effectively, reduce stress, and approach challenges with greater calm and focus. As children grow and continue practicing mindfulness, they will develop valuable skills that will benefit them not only in childhood but throughout their entire lives.

Developing Healthy Relationships with Emotional Intelligence

C hapter 10: Developing Healthy Relationships with Emotional Intelligence

The Role of Emotions in Friendships and Social Interactions

Emotional intelligence (EI) is the ability to recognize, understand, manage, and effectively use emotions in oneself and others. In the context of friendships and social interactions, emotional intelligence plays a pivotal role in helping children build and maintain healthy relationships. Understanding emotions—both their own and those of others—gives children the tools they need to navigate complex social dynamics, resolve conflicts, and foster empathy and connection. Emotional intelligence not only strengthens interpersonal relationships but also builds the foundation for emotional resilience, cooperation, and mutual respect in friendships.

Emotions are at the core of most social interactions, influencing how we communicate, react, and connect with others. In childhood, friendships are often based on shared activities, interests, and positive emotional experiences. However, even among young children, emotions such as jealousy, frustration, disappointment, and anger can complicate friendships. For children to develop healthy relationships, they need to be able to recognize their own emotional responses and understand how those emotions affect their behavior and interactions with peers.

One of the fundamental roles of emotional intelligence in social interactions is emotional awareness—the ability to recognize and label one's emotions. For example, a child who is upset because a friend didn't share a toy might feel anger, disappointment, or sadness. Emotional intelligence helps the child identify these feelings and understand why they are feeling that way. By acknowledging their emotions, the child can begin to express them in a healthy and constructive manner, rather than lashing out or withdrawing. Emotional awareness is the first step toward managing emotions in social settings, allowing children to respond thoughtfully instead of reacting impulsively.

Once children are aware of their emotions, emotion regulation becomes crucial for managing how those emotions are expressed in social interactions. Children with high emotional intelligence learn how to control their emotional responses to fit the situation. For example, a child who feels jealous of a friend's new toy might recognize the emotion and decide to focus on gratitude for their own belongings rather than becoming resentful or trying to take the toy. Emotional regulation helps children maintain control over their behavior, reducing the likelihood of conflicts and helping them navigate difficult feelings without damaging their relationships.

Empathy is another critical component of emotional intelligence that plays a major role in friendships and social interactions. Empathy is the ability to understand and share the feelings of others, which helps children build strong, supportive connections with their peers. For example, if a friend is feeling sad because they weren't invited to a birthday party, an empathetic child might offer comfort, say kind words, or suggest another activity to cheer them up. Empathy not only strengthens friendships by fostering emotional bonds but also helps children develop a sense of compassion and care for others. When children learn to consider the emotions and needs of their peers, they become more likely to engage in cooperative, prosocial behaviors that benefit both parties.

In addition to empathy, perspective-taking is a key aspect of emotional intelligence that enhances social interactions. Perspective-taking involves seeing things from another person's point of view, which helps children understand why their friends might feel or act a certain way. For example, if a child's friend is upset because they lost a game, the child can use perspective-taking to understand that their friend is feeling disappointed, even if the game was just for fun. This understanding helps children respond with kindness and patience, rather than dismissing their friend's feelings or making the situation worse by teasing them. Perspective-taking also encourages conflict resolution, as children can better navigate disagreements by considering the needs and viewpoints of others.

Another important role of emotional intelligence in friendships is effective communication. Emotions often drive how we communicate with others, and children with high emotional intelligence are better able to express their feelings in a clear and respectful way. For example, if a child is feeling frustrated with a friend, they might say, "I'm upset because you didn't listen to me when I was talking," rather than shouting or becoming physically aggressive. This type of communication allows the child to express their emotions without escalating the conflict. At the same time, children with high emotional intelligence are also good listeners, which is a crucial skill for building strong relationships. They can listen to their friends' feelings and needs without interrupting or becoming defensive, which helps create a more open and supportive friendship.

Emotional intelligence also helps children resolve conflicts in friendships. Conflict is a natural part of any relationship, but how children handle conflict can either strengthen or weaken their friendships. Children with high emotional intelligence are more likely to approach conflicts with a problem-solving mindset, looking for solutions that benefit both parties rather than focusing on winning the argument or placing blame. For example, if two friends are arguing over which game to play, a child with emotional intelligence might suggest taking turns or finding a compromise that makes both friends happy. This approach not only resolves the conflict but also reinforces the friendship by showing respect for each other's feelings and needs.

Emotional resilience is another key benefit of emotional intelligence in social interactions. Friendships are not always smooth, and children will inevitably face challenges such as disagreements, disappointments, or moments of feeling left out. Emotional resilience allows children to bounce back from these difficult experiences without becoming overwhelmed by negative emotions. For example, if a child's friend moves away or decides to play with someone else, a child with high emotional resilience can process their feelings of sadness or disappointment and find ways to cope, such as making new friends or focusing on positive memories. This resilience helps children maintain a positive outlook on friendships and continue building healthy relationships even when challenges arise.

In summary, emotional intelligence plays a crucial role in helping children navigate friendships and social interactions. By developing emotional awareness, empathy, perspective-taking, communication skills, and conflict resolution strategies, children are better equipped to form positive, supportive relationships that foster emotional well-being and mutual respect.

Encouraging Positive Social Behaviors

In addition to fostering emotional intelligence, caregivers and educators can actively encourage positive social behaviors that contribute to healthy relationships. Positive social behaviors, such as cooperation, kindness, respect, and inclusivity, are essential for building strong friendships and maintaining harmony in group settings. These behaviors not only help children develop lasting friendships but also promote a sense of community and belonging.

One of the most effective ways to encourage positive social behaviors is through modeling. Children learn a great deal about how to interact with others by observing the adults around them. When caregivers consistently demonstrate positive social behaviors—such as using kind words, offering help, or showing respect for others—children are more likely to imitate those behaviors in their own interactions. For example, a parent who says "please" and "thank you" regularly is teaching their child the importance of politeness and gratitude. Similarly, a teacher who listens attentively to students' concerns is modeling good listening skills, which encourages students to listen to their peers in the same way.

Praise and reinforcement are also key strategies for encouraging positive social behaviors. When children engage in prosocial behaviors—such as sharing a toy, helping a friend, or showing kindness—caregivers can reinforce those behaviors by offering praise and positive feedback. For example, if a child shares their snack with a classmate, a caregiver might say, "That was very generous of you to share with your friend. You made them really happy!" This kind of reinforcement helps children associate positive social behaviors with positive outcomes, making them more likely to repeat those behaviors in the future.

Encouraging cooperation is another important aspect of promoting positive social behaviors. Cooperation involves working together toward a common goal and sharing responsibilities, which helps children develop teamwork skills and fosters a sense of mutual support. Activities that require group collaboration—such as building a project together, playing a team sport, or completing a puzzle—are excellent opportunities for children to practice cooperation. Caregivers can encourage cooperation by emphasizing the importance of working together and helping children resolve any conflicts that arise during group activities. For example, if two children are arguing over how to build a block tower, a caregiver might suggest that they take turns placing the blocks or work together to come up with a new design. Encouraging children to collaborate in this way helps them see the value of cooperation and strengthens their social bonds.

Teaching kindness and empathy is another key component of encouraging positive social behaviors. Children need to learn not only how to recognize their own emotions but also how to respond to the emotions of others with care and understanding. Caregivers can teach kindness and empathy by encouraging children to think about how their actions affect others. For example, if a child is upset because their friend is feeling sad, a caregiver might ask, "What could you do to help your friend feel better?" This prompts the child to think about ways they can show kindness and support, such as offering a hug, saying something nice, or spending time together. Over time, these small acts of kindness help children develop strong empathetic skills and create positive, supportive friendships.

Promoting inclusivity is also essential for fostering positive social behaviors, especially in group settings where children may feel left out or excluded. Inclusivity means making an effort to include everyone, regardless of differences in ability, interests, or background. Caregivers can promote inclusivity by encouraging children to invite others to join in activities and by modeling inclusive language and behavior. For example, if a group of children is playing a game and one child is sitting alone, a caregiver might encourage the group to invite the child to join them, saying, "Let's make sure everyone has a chance to play." This helps children understand that being inclusive is not only kind but also makes group activities more fun and meaningful for everyone involved.

Another way to encourage positive social behaviors is by teaching children effective communication skills. Good communication is the foundation of healthy relationships, and children need to learn how to express their feelings, listen to others, and resolve conflicts in a respectful way. Caregivers can teach communication skills by modeling clear and respectful language, encouraging children to use "I" statements (e.g., "I feel upset when you don't listen to me"), and guiding them through conflict resolution strategies. For example, if two children are arguing, a caregiver might help them communicate their feelings by saying, "Can you tell each other how you're feeling right now?" This encourages the children to express their emotions verbally instead of reacting physically or shutting down. Teaching children how to communicate effectively helps them navigate social challenges and fosters open, honest relationships with their peers.

Conflict resolution is another crucial skill for promoting positive social behaviors. Conflicts are inevitable in any relationship, but how children handle these conflicts can determine whether their relationships are strengthened or damaged. Teaching children constructive conflict resolution strategies—such as listening to each other's perspectives, finding compromises, and apologizing when necessary—helps them resolve disagreements in a way that preserves the relationship. For example, if two children are fighting over a toy, a caregiver might encourage them to take turns, share the toy, or find another activity they both enjoy. By teaching children to approach conflicts with a problem-solving mindset, caregivers help them develop the skills they need to maintain healthy, respectful relationships.

Encouraging emotional expression is another way to support positive social behaviors. Children need to feel comfortable expressing their emotions in order to form genuine connections with others. Caregivers can create a supportive environment by validating children's feelings and encouraging them to talk about their emotions. For instance, if a child is feeling left out by their friends, a caregiver might say, "It sounds like you're feeling sad because you weren't included. It's okay to feel that way. Let's talk about what we can do." This type of validation helps children feel heard and understood, which in turn makes it easier for them to express their emotions in future social situations. When children learn to express their feelings in a healthy way, they are better able to navigate the ups and downs of friendships.

Role-playing and social stories are effective tools for teaching positive social behaviors. Through role-playing, children can practice various social scenarios, such as introducing themselves to a new friend, resolving a disagreement, or asking to join a game. This practice helps children build confidence and reinforces the social skills they need to interact positively with their peers. Social stories, which are short, simple narratives that explain different social situations and appropriate behaviors, can also help children understand how to act in specific scenarios. For example, a social story might explain what to do when a friend is feeling upset, encouraging children to offer comfort or listen without interrupting. Role-playing and social stories make abstract social concepts more concrete for children, giving them a clearer understanding of how to act in different social situations.

Encouraging responsibility in social interactions is another key component of building positive social behaviors. Children need to understand that their actions have consequences, both for themselves and for others. Teaching children to take responsibility for their actions—whether it's apologizing for hurting a friend's feelings or making amends after a disagreement—helps them develop accountability and strengthens their relationships. For example, if a child accidentally knocks over a friend's block tower and the friend becomes upset, a caregiver might guide the child in apologizing and helping rebuild the tower. This teaches the child that taking responsibility for their actions can help repair relationships and foster trust.

Finally, creating opportunities for positive social interactions is essential for encouraging children to practice and develop their social skills. Group activities, cooperative games, and team projects provide children with the chance to work together, communicate, and build relationships in a supportive environment. By participating in these activities, children learn how to share, compromise, and collaborate with their peers. Caregivers can support these interactions by offering guidance and encouragement, helping children navigate any social challenges that arise.

In conclusion, developing healthy relationships with emotional intelligence requires a combination of self-awareness, empathy, communication, and conflict resolution skills. By fostering emotional intelligence and encouraging positive social behaviors, caregivers and educators can help children build strong, supportive friendships and navigate social situations with confidence and compassion. These skills not only benefit children in their current relationships but also lay the foundation for positive social interactions throughout their lives.

Managing Peer Pressure and Bullying

Recognizing Emotional Triggers in Social Settings

Children and adolescents often encounter a wide variety of emotions in social settings, and these emotions can sometimes be challenging to navigate. Peer pressure and bullying, in particular, can trigger intense emotional responses such as fear, anxiety, anger, or sadness. Learning to recognize these emotional triggers is the first step in managing peer pressure and dealing with bullying. Emotional triggers are situations, comments, or behaviors that provoke an emotional reaction. For children, these can be situations where they feel pressure to conform to the group or when they are targeted by a bully, making it difficult for them to manage their emotions in a healthy way.

Peer pressure typically arises when children feel compelled to act in a certain way to fit in with their peers. This pressure might come from friends, classmates, or social groups, and it can lead to behaviors that a child might not otherwise engage in, such as breaking rules, taking risks, or being unkind to others. The fear of being ostracized or ridiculed for not conforming to the group can be a significant emotional trigger. For example, a child might feel anxious or stressed when their friends pressure them to participate in an activity they are uncomfortable with, such as cheating on a test or teasing another student. The emotional pressure to fit in can cloud a child's judgment, making it harder for them to assert their own values and stand up for what they believe in.

Bullying, on the other hand, can evoke even more intense emotional responses, particularly because it often involves repeated harmful behavior that is intended to hurt, humiliate, or intimidate the victim. Bullying can be verbal (name-calling, teasing, threats), physical (hitting, pushing, damaging belongings), or social (excluding someone from a group, spreading rumors). When a child is bullied, they may feel powerless, isolated, or scared. The fear of being targeted can become a constant emotional trigger, leading to increased anxiety, withdrawal from social activities, and even physical symptoms such as headaches or stomachaches. Recognizing these emotional triggers is crucial because it helps children understand how their emotions are being influenced by their social environment, which is the first step in developing strategies to manage their emotional responses.

One of the key emotional triggers in both peer pressure and bullying situations is the fear of rejection. Many children, particularly during adolescence, place a high value on fitting in with their peers. When faced with the possibility of being excluded or rejected, they may experience intense fear or anxiety. This fear can cause them to act against their better judgment in order to avoid social exclusion. For example, a child might join in on teasing another student, even though they know it's wrong, because they are afraid of being left out of the group. The emotional distress caused by this fear can make it difficult for children to think clearly and make decisions that align with their values.

Another common emotional trigger is feelings of insecurity or low self-esteem. Children who feel unsure of themselves or who lack confidence are more vulnerable to peer pressure and bullying. They may feel that they need to prove themselves to others in order to be accepted, which can lead to risky or harmful behaviors. For example, a child with low self-esteem might agree to do something dangerous, like skipping school or experimenting with substances, because they believe it will earn them the approval of their peers. Similarly, children who are bullied may internalize the negative messages they receive from the bully, leading to feelings of worthlessness or self-doubt.

These emotions can make it harder for children to stand up for themselves and resist peer pressure or bullying.

In social settings, children may also experience emotional triggers related to feeling powerless or out of control. When children are pressured by their peers or bullied, they may feel that they have no control over the situation. This sense of powerlessness can lead to frustration, anger, or helplessness, which may manifest in emotional outbursts, withdrawal, or attempts to regain control through aggressive or risky behavior. For example, a child who feels powerless in the face of bullying might lash out at others as a way of coping with their frustration. Recognizing this emotional trigger is important because it can help children understand that they do have choices in how they respond to peer pressure and bullying, even if they feel overwhelmed in the moment.

Social anxiety is another emotional trigger that can make children more susceptible to peer pressure and bullying. Social anxiety occurs when a child feels intense worry or fear about social interactions, particularly in situations where they may be judged or evaluated by others. This anxiety can make it difficult for children to assert themselves or resist peer pressure, as they may be overly concerned with how others perceive them. For example, a child with social anxiety might go along with something they know is wrong because they are afraid of being embarrassed or judged by their peers. Similarly, children who are bullied may experience heightened anxiety in social situations, fearing that they will be targeted or humiliated in front of others.

Anger and frustration can also be emotional triggers in social settings, particularly when a child feels that they are being treated unfairly or unjustly. For example, a child who is being bullied may feel angry about the way they are being treated but may not know how to express that anger in a constructive way. This frustration can lead to emotional outbursts, aggressive behavior, or further isolation from peers. Similarly, a child who is pressured by their friends to do something they are uncomfortable with may feel frustrated by the situation but may not feel confident enough to speak up. Recognizing anger and frustration as emotional triggers can help children understand the root of their emotions and find healthier ways to express and manage those feelings.

By helping children recognize these emotional triggers, caregivers and educators can support them in developing the emotional intelligence needed to navigate peer pressure and bullying. When children are able to identify their emotional responses to social situations, they are better equipped to manage those emotions and make thoughtful decisions about how to respond.

Teaching Kids to Stand Up for Themselves and Others

Standing up for oneself and others is a critical skill for children, particularly in the context of peer pressure and bullying. However, it can be difficult for children to assert themselves, especially when they fear social consequences or are unsure of how to respond. Teaching children how to stand up for themselves and others in a confident and respectful way helps them resist peer pressure, deal with bullying, and foster a sense of empowerment and self-respect.

One of the most important aspects of standing up for oneself is assertiveness. Assertiveness is the ability to express one's thoughts, feelings, and needs in a direct and respectful manner. Unlike passive behavior, which involves giving in to others or avoiding confrontation, assertiveness allows children to communicate their boundaries and stand up for their rights without being aggressive or hostile. Teaching children assertiveness skills helps them resist peer pressure by giving them the confidence to say no when they are uncomfortable or when something goes against their values. For example, if a child is being pressured to participate in a risky activity, assertiveness allows them to say, "No, I'm not comfortable with that," in a firm but respectful tone.

One way to teach assertiveness is by using role-playing exercises. Caregivers and educators can create scenarios in which children practice standing up for themselves in different situations, such as being pressured by peers to break a rule or being teased by a bully. In these role-playing exercises, children can practice using assertive language, such as "I don't like it when you say that," or "Please stop, that's not okay." Role-playing helps children build confidence in their ability to assert themselves and provides them with practical tools for responding to peer pressure and bullying.

In addition to assertiveness, it's important to teach children self-advocacy— the ability to stand up for their own needs and rights. Self-advocacy involves knowing one's boundaries, understanding one's rights, and speaking up when those boundaries or rights are violated. For example, if a child is being bullied at school, they need to know that it is their right to feel safe and respected, and they should be encouraged to seek help from a trusted adult if the bullying continues. Teaching children to advocate for themselves helps them feel empowered to take action when they are being mistreated, rather than feeling helpless or resigned to the situation.

Another important aspect of standing up for oneself is building self-confidence. Children who are confident in themselves are less likely to give in to peer pressure or tolerate bullying. Caregivers and educators can help children build self-confidence by offering positive reinforcement, encouraging them to pursue their interests and strengths, and helping them develop a strong sense of identity. When children feel good about who they are and what they stand for, they are more likely to resist pressure to conform to negative behaviors and more likely to stand up for what they believe in.

Teaching children to stand up for others, not just themselves, is equally important in combating peer pressure and bullying. Bystander intervention is the practice of stepping in to support someone who is being mistreated or bullied. Children often witness bullying or peer pressure in their social circles, and teaching them to stand up for their peers can create a more inclusive and supportive environment. For example, if a child sees a classmate being teased, they can intervene by saying, "That's not funny. Please stop." Standing up for others not only helps the victim but also sends a message that bullying and peer pressure are not acceptable behaviors.

Bystander intervention can be taught through empathy-building exercises that encourage children to consider how others feel when they are being mistreated. Caregivers can ask children questions like, "How would you feel if someone did that to you?" or "What can you do to help your friend feel safe?" These questions help children develop empathy for their peers and understand the importance of standing up for others. Additionally, by teaching children to stand together against bullying and peer pressure, caregivers can help create a culture of support and mutual respect within their social circles. When children see their peers standing up for others, they are more likely to do the same, reinforcing positive social norms and reducing the power of bullies and peer pressure.

Teaching refusal skills is another key component of standing up against peer pressure. Many children struggle to say no when they feel pressured by their friends or social group, often out of fear of rejection or ridicule. Refusal skills provide children with the tools to assertively decline participation in activities they are uncomfortable with or that go against their values. These skills can be taught by modeling specific language, such as, "No thanks, I'm not interested," or, "I don't want to do that." Refusal skills also include the ability to offer alternatives, such as, "Why don't we do something else instead?" or, "Let's find a different way to have fun." This approach gives children the confidence to resist peer pressure without feeling like they have to confront or alienate their peers.

Encouraging critical thinking is another important aspect of teaching children to resist peer pressure. Children need to be able to think critically about the consequences of their actions and whether those actions align with their values and goals. For example, a child who is being pressured to break a rule at school should be encouraged to consider the potential consequences of that action—such as getting into trouble or losing trust—and weigh those consequences against the temporary approval they might gain from their peers. Teaching children to think critically about the long-term impact of their decisions helps them make more thoughtful choices in the face of peer pressure.

Building a support network is also vital for helping children stand up for themselves and others. Children need to know that they have trusted adults—such as parents, teachers, or counselors—whom they can turn to for guidance and support. Caregivers can encourage children to reach out to these trusted individuals when they are facing peer pressure or bullying. By knowing that they have a support system, children feel less isolated and more empowered to stand up for themselves. Caregivers can also encourage children to surround themselves with positive friends who respect their boundaries and values, as having a group of supportive peers can make it easier to resist negative influences.

Promoting positive self-talk is another effective strategy for helping children stand up to peer pressure and bullying. Negative self-talk—such as thinking, "I'm not strong enough to say no," or, "Everyone will hate me if I stand up for myself"—can undermine a child's ability to assert their needs and values. Teaching children to replace negative thoughts with positive affirmations—such as, "I have the right to say no," or, "I'm brave for standing up for what's right"—can help build their confidence and resilience in difficult situations. Encouraging children to practice positive self-talk before and after challenging social interactions can strengthen their ability to stand up for themselves in the future.

Developing coping strategies for dealing with the emotional aftermath of peer pressure and bullying is also important. Even when children successfully stand up for themselves or others, they may still experience emotional distress, such as feelings of anxiety, guilt, or frustration. Teaching children healthy coping strategies—such as talking to a trusted adult, journalism about their feelings, or engaging in calming activities like deep breathing or exercise—can help them process these emotions and regain their emotional balance. Caregivers can also remind children that it's normal to feel upset or conflicted after standing up to peer pressure or bullying, and that seeking support from others is a sign of strength, not weakness.

Recognizing when to seek help is another important skill for children who are dealing with peer pressure or bullying. While standing up for oneself and others is important, there are situations where children may need additional support from adults. For example, if bullying becomes persistent or escalates into physical harm or severe emotional distress, children should be encouraged to seek help from a teacher, school counselor, or parent. Caregivers can teach children how to recognize the signs that they need help—such as feeling overwhelmed, unsafe, or unable to cope with the situation—and assure them that it's okay to ask for help when needed.

Additionally, it's important to teach children the difference between being assertive and being aggressive. While standing up for oneself is important, it should be done in a way that is respectful and constructive. Aggressive responses—such as yelling, name-calling, or physically retaliating—can escalate the situation and lead to further conflict. Caregivers can help children practice assertive communication, which involves expressing their feelings and needs clearly and calmly, without resorting to aggression or hostility. For example, a child might say, "I don't like it when you tease me, and I want you to stop," rather than responding with insults or physical actions. Teaching children to remain calm and assertive in difficult situations helps them maintain control over their emotions and de-escalate conflicts.

Finally, it's important to create a safe and open environment where children feel comfortable discussing their experiences with peer pressure and bullying. Caregivers should encourage open communication by regularly checking in with children about their social interactions and emotions. Asking open-ended questions like, "How do you feel about your friends at school?" or, "Has anyone ever pressured you to do something you didn't want to do?" can provide valuable insight into the challenges children may be facing. By creating a space where children feel heard and supported, caregivers can help them develop the confidence and resilience needed to stand up to peer pressure and bullying.

In conclusion, recognizing emotional triggers in social settings is the first step in helping children manage peer pressure and bullying. By teaching children to stand up for themselves and others through assertiveness, self-advocacy, empathy, and critical thinking, caregivers and educators can equip them with the tools they need to navigate these challenges with confidence and resilience. With the right support, children can learn to assert their values, protect their well-being, and foster a positive social environment that discourages bullying and promotes healthy peer interactions.

Modeling Emotional Intelligence at Home

How Parents Can Set the Emotional Tone

Parents play a crucial role in shaping the emotional lives of their children. From a very young age, children learn how to manage their emotions by observing their parents' behaviors, reactions, and interactions with others. The home environment serves as the first and most consistent emotional landscape for children, and the tone set by parents greatly influences how children develop their own emotional intelligence (EI). Emotional intelligence encompasses the ability to recognize, understand, and manage one's own emotions, as well as the ability to empathize with others and navigate social complexities. By modeling emotional intelligence in everyday interactions, parents can help their children build the foundation for a lifetime of emotional well-being and healthy relationships.

Parents set the emotional tone at home through both their verbal and non-verbal behaviors. Every interaction—whether it's a calm discussion or a heated disagreement—teaches children how to handle emotions. When parents model calmness, patience, and empathy in their own emotional responses, they demonstrate to their children how to handle difficult emotions in healthy ways. On the other hand, if parents frequently react with anger, frustration, or withdrawal, children may learn to imitate these behaviors when they encounter their own emotional challenges.

One of the key ways that parents can set a positive emotional tone is by practicing emotional regulation themselves. Children are constantly watching how their parents respond to stress, frustration, or disappointment. For example, when a parent encounters a stressful situation, such as running late for an appointment, they have the opportunity to model emotional regulation by remaining calm and using strategies like deep breathing or positive self-talk. If a parent instead reacts by yelling or becoming overwhelmed, children may learn that this is the appropriate way to handle stress. Conversely, when parents model emotional regulation, they show children that while strong emotions are a normal part of life, they can be managed in a thoughtful and constructive manner.

Additionally, parents set the emotional tone by creating an environment of emotional safety at home. Emotional safety means that children feel secure in expressing their emotions without fear of judgment, criticism, or punishment. When parents encourage open and honest communication about emotions, children learn that it's okay to have a wide range of feelings, including anger, sadness, or frustration. For example, when a child comes home from school feeling upset because they had a disagreement with a friend, a parent can create emotional safety by listening without interrupting, validating the child's feelings, and offering support. This response shows the child that their emotions are important and worthy of attention, fostering emotional intelligence by teaching the child how to recognize and express their feelings.

Another important aspect of setting the emotional tone is modeling empathy in everyday interactions. Empathy is the ability to understand and share the feelings of others, and it is a critical component of emotional intelligence. Parents can model empathy by showing care and concern for others, both within the family and in broader social contexts. For example, if a parent sees someone struggling, they might express compassion by saying, "That person looks like they're having a tough day. I hope things get better for them." This models for the child how to recognize and respond to the emotions of others. Within the family, parents can model empathy by acknowledging the emotions of their children and responding with warmth and understanding.

For example, if a child is feeling anxious about an upcoming test, a parent might say, "I understand that you're feeling nervous. Tests can be stressful, but I'm proud of how hard you've been studying." This empathetic response not only validates the child's feelings but also shows them how to approach the emotions of others with kindness and support.

Parents can also set the emotional tone by practicing positive communication and conflict resolution at home. Disagreements and conflicts are a natural part of family life, but how parents handle these conflicts teaches children valuable lessons about emotional regulation and social interactions. When parents approach conflicts with a problem-solving mindset—listening to each other's perspectives, staying calm, and working together to find solutions—they model constructive ways of managing disagreements. For example, if two siblings are arguing over a toy, a parent can intervene by helping them express their feelings ("I understand you're both upset because you want to play with the same toy") and guiding them toward a solution that works for both parties, such as taking turns. This teaches children that conflicts can be resolved through communication and compromise, rather than through aggression or avoidance.

Self-awareness is another critical element of emotional intelligence that parents can model for their children. Self-awareness involves recognizing one's own emotions and understanding how those emotions influence behavior. Parents can model self-awareness by reflecting on their own emotions and sharing their thoughts with their children. For example, a parent might say, "I'm feeling really frustrated right now because I had a difficult day at work. I'm going to take a few minutes to relax before we talk about it." This models for the child that it's okay to acknowledge and express emotions, and that taking time to process feelings can help prevent emotional outbursts. By being open about their own emotional experiences, parents can help children develop the self-awareness needed to recognize and manage their own emotions.

It's also important for parents to model emotional resilience—the ability to bounce back from challenges and setbacks. Life is full of ups and downs, and children learn how to navigate these experiences by observing how their parents respond to adversity. When parents model resilience—by staying optimistic, maintaining a sense of perspective, and finding constructive ways to cope with difficulties—they teach their children that challenges are a normal part of life and that emotions, while sometimes difficult, can be managed. For example, if a parent loses their job, they might model resilience by expressing their disappointment but also focusing on finding new opportunities and staying hopeful about the future. This teaches children that while it's okay to feel sad or discouraged in difficult times, it's also important to stay focused on solutions and maintain a positive outlook.

In sum, parents play a powerful role in setting the emotional tone at home through their behaviors, responses, and interactions. By modeling emotional regulation, empathy, positive communication, self-awareness, and resilience, parents create an environment where emotional intelligence can thrive, giving their children the tools they need to navigate their own emotions and social relationships with confidence and care.

Being an Emotion Coach for Your Child

In addition to modeling emotional intelligence, parents can take on the role of emotion coaches for their children, actively teaching them how to recognize, understand, and manage their emotions. Emotion coaching involves guiding children through their emotional experiences, helping them navigate difficult feelings, and providing them with strategies to cope with challenges in a healthy way. As an emotion coach, a parent helps their child develop emotional intelligence by offering support, validation, and practical tools for managing emotions.

The first step in being an effective emotion coach is recognizing your child's emotions, even when they aren't explicitly expressed. Children, especially younger ones, may not always have the vocabulary or awareness to identify their emotions, and they may express their feelings through behaviors such as tantrums, withdrawal, or aggression. As an emotion coach, it's important to look beyond the behavior and try to understand the underlying emotion. For example, if a child is throwing a tantrum after losing a game, the parent might recognize that the child is feeling frustrated or disappointed, even if the child hasn't said so. By acknowledging the emotion behind the behavior, the parent can help the child feel understood and supported.

Once the emotion has been identified, the next step is to validate the child's feelings. Validation involves acknowledging and accepting the child's emotions without judgment or criticism. This teaches the child that all emotions are valid and that it's okay to feel sad, angry, or frustrated. For example, a parent might say, "I can see that you're feeling really angry right now because your sister took your toy. It's okay to feel upset about that." By validating the child's emotions, the parent helps the child feel heard and understood, which is the first step toward emotional regulation.

After validating the child's feelings, an emotion coach helps the child label their emotions. Emotion labeling is a critical part of emotional intelligence because it helps children develop the vocabulary they need to express their feelings. For example, a parent might say, "It seems like you're feeling frustrated because you're having a hard time with your homework." This not only helps the child understand what they are feeling but also gives them the language to express their emotions in the future. Emotion labeling is especially important for younger children, who may not yet have the words to describe their emotional experiences. By teaching children to name their emotions, parents help them gain a deeper understanding of their internal world, making it easier for them to manage their feelings.

Once the child's emotions have been identified and labeled, the next step is to teach coping strategies. As an emotion coach, a parent can help their child develop a toolkit of coping strategies for managing difficult emotions.

These strategies might include deep breathing, taking a break, practicing mindfulness, or engaging in a calming activity like drawing or listening to music. For example, if a child is feeling overwhelmed by frustration during homework time, the parent might suggest taking a few deep breaths or stepping away from the homework for a short break. Over time, these strategies become internalized, allowing the child to manage their emotions more independently. The goal of emotion coaching is not to fix or eliminate the child's emotions but to give them the tools they need to cope with their feelings in a healthy way.

Problem-solving is another important component of emotion coaching. Once the child has calmed down and is ready to engage, the parent can help them think through solutions to the problem that triggered the emotion. For example, if a child is feeling upset because a friend didn't invite them to a party, the parent can guide the child through a problem-solving process by asking questions like, "What can you do to feel better about this situation?. They might explore various options together, such as talking to the friend, inviting the friend to another activity, or focusing on other fun things to do instead. The key to effective problem-solving is to help the child understand that while emotions are a natural part of life, they don't have to control their actions. By teaching children to think through challenges and consider different solutions, parents empower them to take control of difficult situations rather than becoming overwhelmed by their emotions.

In addition to teaching problem-solving skills, emotion coaching also involves setting limits on inappropriate behavior. While all emotions are valid, not all behaviors are acceptable. As an emotion coach, it's important to teach children that while it's okay to feel angry, sad, or frustrated, it's not okay to act out in harmful ways, such as hitting, yelling, or throwing things. For example, if a child lashes out in anger, the parent might say, "I understand that you're feeling really angry right now, and that's okay. But it's not okay to hit your brother. Let's find another way to handle your anger." By setting clear boundaries and helping the child find alternative ways to express their emotions, parents teach emotional regulation in a structured and compassionate way.

Another key aspect of emotion coaching is teaching empathy. Empathy is a critical part of emotional intelligence because it helps children understand and respond to the emotions of others. Parents can model empathy by acknowledging their child's emotions and responding with care and concern, but they can also teach children to practice empathy in their relationships with others. For example, if a sibling is upset, a parent might encourage their child to think about how their sibling is feeling and suggest ways to offer comfort or support. By guiding children to recognize and respond to the emotions of others, parents help them develop the empathy needed to build strong, compassionate relationships.

It's also important for emotion coaches to be patient and consistent. Emotional intelligence is a skill that develops over time, and children will need plenty of practice to become adept at managing their emotions. Parents should expect that their children will make mistakes and experience setbacks, especially when they are dealing with strong or unfamiliar emotions. For example, a child who is learning to cope with frustration may continue to have occasional tantrums, even after practicing calming strategies. In these moments, it's important for parents to remain patient, offer support, and reinforce the lessons of emotional regulation. Consistency is key—when children see that their parents are reliably available to help them navigate their emotions, they will feel more secure and confident in their ability to manage those emotions on their own.

Emotion coaching also involves encouraging reflection after emotional episodes have passed. Once a child has calmed down, parents can gently guide them in reflecting on what happened and what they can learn from the experience. For example, after a tantrum, a parent might say, "What do you think made you so upset earlier? Is there something we can do differently next time?" This type of reflection helps children become more aware of their emotional triggers and reinforces the idea that they can learn from their emotional experiences. Over time, this process of reflection helps children become more self-aware and better equipped to handle similar situations in the future.

Incorporating daily routines that support emotional intelligence is another effective strategy for emotion coaching. For example, parents can create regular opportunities for children to talk about their feelings, such as during family meals or bedtime. Asking questions like, "What was the best part of your day? What was the hardest part?" encourages children to reflect on their emotions in a safe and supportive environment. Parents can also introduce simple mindfulness practices, such as deep breathing or guided relaxation, into the daily routine to help children develop emotional regulation skills. By making emotional intelligence a regular part of family life, parents help their children develop the habits and skills they need to navigate their emotions with confidence and ease.

Celebrating emotional growth and successes is also an important part of emotion coaching. When children successfully manage their emotions or handle a difficult situation in a positive way, it's important for parents to recognize and celebrate those accomplishments. For example, if a child uses calming strategies to manage their frustration during a challenging homework assignment, a parent might say, "I'm really proud of how you handled your frustration today. You took a deep breath and kept going, and that's not easy to do!" Celebrating emotional growth reinforces the child's efforts and helps them build self-confidence in their ability to manage their emotions. This positive reinforcement encourages children to continue practicing emotional intelligence and developing resilience in the face of challenges.

Finally, it's important for parents to remember that emotion coaching is a partnership. While parents play a guiding role in helping their children develop emotional intelligence, the process is collaborative. Parents should aim to work with their children, rather than simply directing them. This means actively listening to the child's thoughts and feelings, offering guidance and support without being overly controlling, and respecting the child's individual emotional journey. Every child is unique, and emotion coaching should be tailored to meet the specific needs, temperament, and developmental stage of each child. By working together, parents and children can build a strong foundation of emotional intelligence that will serve them well throughout life.

In conclusion, being an emotion coach for your child involves recognizing and validating their emotions, teaching emotional vocabulary, offering coping strategies, and guiding them through problem-solving. It also requires setting limits on inappropriate behavior, modeling empathy, encouraging reflection, and celebrating emotional growth. Through patience, consistency, and a collaborative approach, parents can help their children develop the emotional intelligence they need to navigate their feelings, build healthy relationships, and face life's challenges with resilience and confidence. Emotion coaching is not just a one-time effort but a continuous process that evolves as children grow, giving them the tools to manage their emotions and thrive emotionally, socially, and intellectually.

Emotional Intelligence in the Classroom

Creating Emotionally Intelligent Classrooms

Emotional intelligence (EI) plays an increasingly significant role in today's classrooms, where the ability to manage emotions, empathize with others, and navigate social interactions is just as important as academic success. Creating an emotionally intelligent classroom involves fostering an environment where students feel safe to express their emotions, where empathy and understanding are promoted, and where emotional regulation is integrated into everyday learning. Classrooms that focus on emotional intelligence encourage students not only to thrive academically but also to develop the social and emotional skills necessary for lifelong success.

To create an emotionally intelligent classroom, the first step is to establish a culture of emotional safety and openness. Emotional safety means that students feel comfortable sharing their thoughts and feelings without fear of judgment or ridicule. This type of environment fosters trust between students and teachers, making students more likely to participate in class discussions, seek help when they need it, and take risks in their learning. Teachers can create emotional safety by setting clear expectations for respectful communication, modeling empathy and understanding, and providing positive reinforcement when students express their emotions in healthy ways.

One effective way to establish emotional safety is to normalize conversations about emotions. In many classrooms, emotions are often overlooked or dismissed in favor of academic instruction, but integrating emotional discussions into the daily routine helps students become more comfortable with their feelings. For example, teachers can start the day with a check-in, asking students how they're feeling and giving them the opportunity to share their emotions in a supportive environment. Questions like "What's something that made you happy today?" or "What's something that was challenging for you?" invite students to reflect on their emotional experiences and build emotional awareness.

Creating an emotionally intelligent classroom also requires fostering empathy among students. Empathy is the ability to understand and share the feelings of others, and it is a key component of emotional intelligence. Teachers can promote empathy by encouraging students to listen to one another, recognize different perspectives, and respond to the emotions of their peers with kindness and support. For example, when a student is upset or struggling, the teacher can use the situation as a teaching moment by asking the class, "How do you think your classmate might be feeling right now? What can we do to help them?" This not only helps the individual student feel supported but also teaches the entire class the value of empathy and compassionate behavior.

Modeling emotional intelligence is another essential component of creating an emotionally intelligent classroom. Teachers serve as role models for their students, and the way they handle their own emotions sets an example for how students should manage theirs. When teachers model emotional regulation, empathy, and positive communication, they provide students with a real-life example of emotional intelligence in action. For example, if a teacher is feeling frustrated due to a challenging classroom situation, they can model emotional regulation by calmly explaining their feelings and taking a moment to breathe or collect their thoughts. This demonstrates to students that emotions, even difficult ones, can be managed in a healthy way.

In addition to modeling emotional intelligence, teachers can explicitly teach emotional skills as part of the curriculum. Emotional intelligence skills, such as recognizing and labeling emotions, regulating emotional responses, and resolving conflicts, are just as important as academic skills and should be taught with the same level of attention. Incorporating social-emotional learning (SEL) into the classroom helps students build the skills they need to manage their emotions, interact with others, and navigate challenges. This can be done through structured lessons on topics like emotional regulation, empathy, and relationship-building, as well as through informal discussions about emotions during regular classroom activities.

Another important aspect of creating an emotionally intelligent classroom is teaching conflict resolution. Conflicts are a natural part of any social environment, including the classroom, and students need to learn how to manage disagreements in a constructive and respectful way. Teachers can teach conflict resolution skills by guiding students through the process of identifying the problem, expressing their feelings, listening to the perspectives of others, and finding a solution that works for everyone involved. For example, if two students are arguing over a shared resource, the teacher can encourage them to use "I" statements (e.g., "I feel upset because I didn't get a turn") and help them brainstorm a compromise, such as taking turns or sharing the resource. Teaching students how to resolve conflicts peacefully not only improves the classroom environment but also equips students with valuable life skills.

In an emotionally intelligent classroom, it's also important to recognize and celebrate emotional growth. Just as academic progress is celebrated, emotional milestones should be acknowledged and reinforced. For example, when a student successfully manages their frustration during a difficult task or shows kindness to a classmate who is upset, the teacher can offer positive feedback, such as, "I noticed how patient you were when you felt frustrated today. That's a great way to handle your emotions." Recognizing emotional growth helps students feel proud of their emotional development and encourages them to continue practicing emotional intelligence.

Finally, an emotionally intelligent classroom is one that values inclusivity and respect for diversity. Emotional intelligence involves recognizing and respecting the emotions and experiences of others, and this extends to respecting cultural, racial, and individual differences. Teachers can foster an inclusive classroom environment by encouraging students to appreciate the diverse perspectives and experiences of their peers. This might involve teaching students about different cultural practices, facilitating discussions about identity and belonging, or creating opportunities for students to share their own experiences and learn from one another. An inclusive classroom not only promotes emotional intelligence but also helps students feel a sense of belonging and acceptance, which is critical for their emotional and social development.

Activities and Resources for Teachers

Integrating emotional intelligence into the classroom doesn't have to be complicated. There are many activities and resources that teachers can use to help students develop emotional skills in fun and engaging ways. These activities not only teach emotional intelligence but also promote a positive and supportive classroom environment.

1. Emotion Check-In

One simple and effective activity is to start the day with an emotion check-in. Teachers can create a chart with different emotions (happy, sad, frustrated, excited, etc.) and ask students to place their name or a marker next to the emotion they are feeling that day. This activity helps students become more aware of their emotions and gives the teacher a sense of how the class is feeling. It also provides an opportunity for students to discuss their feelings with the teacher or their peers if they need support.

2. Feelings Wheel

A feelings wheel is a tool that helps students expand their emotional vocabulary and better understand the nuances of their emotions. The wheel contains different categories of emotions, such as joy, anger, sadness, and fear, with subcategories that describe more specific emotions. For example, under "anger," there might be feelings such as frustration, irritation, or resentment. Teachers can use the feelings wheel to help students identify and label their emotions during discussions or after a conflict. This activity encourages emotional awareness and helps students articulate their feelings more precisely.

3. Role-Playing Scenarios

Role-playing is a great way to teach emotional intelligence through experiential learning. Teachers can create role-playing scenarios that involve common classroom situations, such as resolving a conflict, standing up for a friend, or dealing with disappointment. For example, one role-playing scenario might involve two students working together on a project, but one student feels frustrated because they aren't being listened to. The students can act out how to express their feelings and work toward a solution. Role-playing helps students practice emotional regulation, empathy, and communication skills in a safe and controlled environment.

4. Mindfulness Practices

Mindfulness is a valuable tool for teaching emotional regulation and focus. Teachers can introduce mindfulness practices into the classroom to help students manage their emotions and reduce stress. One simple mindfulness activity is a mindful breathing exercise, where students are guided to focus on their breath and calm their minds. Teachers can start with short, guided mindfulness sessions of one to five minutes and gradually increase the time as students become more comfortable with the practice. These exercises help students center themselves, stay focused, and manage their emotions throughout the school day.

5. Empathy Mapping

An empathy mapping activity helps students understand the emotions and perspectives of others. In this activity, teachers ask students to think about a character from a book, a historical figure, or even a classmate who is going through a challenging situation. Students then create an empathy map by answering questions such as, "What is this person feeling?" "What are they thinking?" and "What do they need from others?" This activity encourages students to put themselves in someone else's shoes and think about how emotions influence behavior. It's an excellent way to foster empathy and deepen emotional understanding.

6. Emotion Journals

Emotion journals give students a private space to reflect on their emotions and experiences. Teachers can encourage students to write about their feelings in a journal, particularly after significant emotional events, such as a conflict with a peer or a challenging test. Prompts such as "How did you feel today?" "What made you happy or upset?" and "What would you do differently next time?" help guide students' reflections. Journalism allows students to process their emotions in a thoughtful way and can lead to greater emotional awareness and self-regulation.

7. Classroom Calm-Down Corner

A calm-down corner is a designated space in the classroom where students can go to regulate their emotions when they feel overwhelmed. This space can include calming tools such as stress balls, coloring books, fidget toys, or a glitter jar, along with posters that offer calming strategies like deep breathing or positive self-talk. When a student is feeling upset or stressed, they can use the calm-down corner to take a break, collect their thoughts, and return to class feeling more centered. This gives students a constructive way to manage their emotions without disrupting the learning environment.

8. Group Problem-Solving Discussions

Teachers can facilitate group problem-solving discussions where students work together to address common emotional or social challenges. In these discussions, students can be presented with hypothetical scenarios or real-life issues they may encounter, such as handling peer disagreements, dealing with exclusion, or managing stress before a test. The teacher guides the students through the process of identifying the problem, discussing the emotions involved, and brainstorming possible solutions. This activity not only teaches problem-solving skills but also promotes empathy and collaboration, as students listen to each other's perspectives and work together to find solutions.

For example, the teacher might pose a question like, "What would you do if you saw a classmate being left out during recess?" The students can then discuss how they would feel in that situation, what they could do to help, and how they could approach the person who is excluding their classmate. This group discussion encourages students to think critically about social dynamics and emotional responses, helping them develop both social and emotional intelligence.

9. Literature and Emotional Intelligence

Another effective way to teach emotional intelligence in the classroom is through literature and storytelling. Books and stories often explore complex emotions and relationships, providing an excellent opportunity for students to learn about empathy, emotional regulation, and social interactions. Teachers can select books that feature characters experiencing a range of emotions and challenges and use these stories as a basis for discussion. After reading a book or story, teachers can ask students questions such as, "How do you think the character was feeling?" "What could they have done differently?" and "How did their emotions affect their choices?"

For younger students, picture books that focus on emotions can help them better understand their own feelings and the feelings of others. For older students, novels and biographies offer more nuanced examples of emotional intelligence in action, allowing for deeper discussions about character motivations, empathy, and emotional growth. Literature serves as a powerful tool for teaching emotional intelligence because it allows students to explore emotions in a safe and engaging way, all while enhancing their literacy skills.

10. Emotional Vocabulary Building

Building a strong emotional vocabulary is essential for emotional intelligence, as it allows students to accurately identify and express their emotions. Teachers can use emotional vocabulary-building activities to help students expand their understanding of different emotions and how to articulate them. For instance, a teacher might create a word wall with a variety of emotions, from basic feelings like "happy" and "sad" to more complex emotions like "disappointed," "overwhelmed," or "anxious."

Throughout the school day, teachers can encourage students to use these words to describe their feelings. For example, during a group discussion, a teacher might say, "Can anyone think of a word on our emotions wall that describes how the character felt when they lost the game?" This helps students practice using specific emotional language, making it easier for them to communicate their feelings effectively.

11. Social-Emotional Learning Programs

There are many structured social-emotional learning (SEL) programs that provide teachers with resources and activities to teach emotional intelligence in the classroom. Programs like CASEL (Collaborative for Academic, Social, and Emotional Learning), Second Step, and Zones of Regulation offer comprehensive curricula designed to teach students emotional awareness, empathy, emotional regulation, and social skills. These programs often include lesson plans, worksheets, role-playing exercises, and reflection activities that help students practice emotional intelligence in a structured and supportive way.

Teachers can integrate these programs into their regular classroom routines or use them as part of a dedicated SEL curriculum. SEL programs provide valuable guidance for teachers who are looking for ways to incorporate emotional intelligence into their teaching while aligning with educational standards.

12. "What Would You Do?" Scenarios

The "What Would You Do?" game is an interactive way to engage students in thinking critically about emotional and social situations. Teachers can present students with different scenarios, such as "What would you do if your friend was upset because they didn't do well on a test?" or "What would you do if someone teased you on the playground?" Students can take turns responding to these scenarios and discussing the emotions involved, as well as the best ways to handle the situation.

This activity encourages students to practice empathy, emotional regulation, and problem-solving in a fun and engaging way. It also helps students develop greater confidence in their ability to handle real-life emotional challenges.

13. Gratitude Journals

Practicing gratitude is a powerful way to boost emotional well-being and foster a positive classroom environment. Teachers can introduce gratitude journals as a daily or weekly activity, where students write down things they are thankful for. This practice helps students focus on the positive aspects of their lives, even during challenging times, and encourages them to develop a mindset of appreciation and optimism.

Gratitude journals can also be used to reflect on social and emotional experiences. For example, teachers might ask students to write about a time when a friend helped them or a moment when they felt proud of themselves for showing kindness. Over time, this practice helps students build emotional resilience and a greater sense of well-being.

14. Peer Support and Mentoring Programs

Peer support programs and mentoring are excellent ways to build emotional intelligence within the classroom community. In a peer mentoring program, older or more experienced students can be paired with younger students to offer guidance and support. These relationships provide opportunities for students to practice empathy, active listening, and emotional support in a structured and supervised environment.

For example, mentors can help younger students navigate social challenges, such as resolving conflicts with friends or managing academic stress. Peer mentoring not only helps the younger students but also benefits the mentors by giving them the opportunity to develop leadership skills and deepen their emotional intelligence.

15. Emotional Intelligence Games and Apps

There are many educational games and apps designed to teach emotional intelligence skills in an interactive and engaging way. These digital resources can be integrated into classroom activities or used as part of an emotional intelligence curriculum. For example, apps like "Smiling Mind" or "Breathe, Think, Do" help students practice mindfulness, emotional regulation, and problem-solving.

Teachers can also use online resources such as emotion recognition games, where students practice identifying emotions based on facial expressions or social cues. These games provide a fun and effective way for students to build emotional awareness and empathy.

In conclusion, creating an emotionally intelligent classroom requires a commitment to fostering emotional awareness, empathy, and emotional regulation through both structured lessons and everyday interactions. By integrating activities like role-playing, mindfulness, literature discussions, and social-emotional learning programs, teachers can provide students with the tools they need to succeed not only academically but also emotionally and socially. Emotionally intelligent classrooms help students build the skills they need to navigate their feelings, resolve conflicts, and create positive, supportive relationships, both in school and beyond.

Digital Age Challenges: Managing Screen Time and Emotions

How Technology Affects Emotional Development

In today's rapidly evolving digital landscape, technology has become an integral part of children's and adolescents' daily lives. From smartphones and tablets to social media and video games, children are exposed to technology at a younger age and for longer periods than ever before. While technology offers many benefits, such as access to educational resources, communication tools, and entertainment, it also presents significant challenges to emotional development. The effects of excessive screen time on children's emotional well-being and interpersonal skills have become a growing concern for parents, educators, and mental health professionals.

Technology's impact on emotional development can be both direct and indirect. Directly, it affects how children and adolescents experience and process emotions, as well as how they interact with others in social settings. Indirectly, it influences emotional health by affecting cognitive functions such as attention span, impulse control, and problem-solving skills—factors that are closely tied to emotional regulation.

One of the primary ways that technology affects emotional development is through its influence on social interactions. Many children today spend significant amounts of time communicating through digital platforms such as texting, social media, or online gaming. While these platforms can help children stay connected with peers and family, they often lack the emotional richness of face-to-face communication. In-person interactions allow children to read non-verbal cues such as facial expressions, body language, and tone of voice, which are essential for developing empathy and understanding others' emotions. However, digital communication tends to be more limited, often leading to misunderstandings or shallow connections.

For example, when children communicate through text or social media, they may miss the emotional nuances that come with hearing someone's voice or seeing their facial expression. This can make it harder for them to develop empathy, as they are not fully exposed to the emotional context of the conversation. Over time, reliance on digital communication may hinder children's ability to recognize and respond to others' emotions, a key component of emotional intelligence.

Furthermore, social media platforms, in particular, can exacerbate emotional challenges by creating unrealistic standards of beauty, success, and happiness. Children and adolescents are often bombarded with carefully curated images and stories that present an idealized version of life. These comparisons can lead to feelings of inadequacy, low self-esteem, and social anxiety, as children may feel that they are not living up to the perceived standards of their peers. For example, a child who frequently sees photos of their friends attending parties or achieving success may feel left out or inadequate, even if their own life is full of positive experiences. This phenomenon, known as "social comparison," can contribute to feelings of loneliness and depression, especially during adolescence when social validation becomes increasingly important.

Technology also affects emotional development through the over stimulation that comes with excessive screen time. Many digital activities, such as video games, social media, and online videos, are designed to capture and maintain attention by providing constant stimulation and instant gratification. For example, video games often feature fast-paced action, bright colors, and rewards that encourage players to keep playing. Similarly, social media platforms use notifications, likes, and comments to keep users engaged. While these features can be entertaining, they can also make it harder for children to focus on less stimulating activities, such as reading, doing homework, or engaging in face-to-face conversations. This over stimulation can affect children's ability to regulate their emotions, as they may become more impatient, easily frustrated, or prone to emotional outbursts when they are not receiving constant feedback or rewards.

Moreover, the constant availability of technology can interfere with important aspects of emotional development, such as self-reflection, mindfulness, and boredom. Before the digital age, children had more opportunities to experience unstructured time, which allowed them to explore their thoughts, emotions, and imagination. However, with smartphones and tablets always within reach, children are now less likely to experience downtime. Instead of reflecting on their day, processing their emotions, or engaging in creative play, they may turn to their devices for instant entertainment or distraction. This can prevent children from developing the emotional resilience and coping skills that come from navigating boredom, frustration, or difficult emotions on their own.

Sleep disruption is another significant way that technology affects emotional development. Many children and adolescents use their devices late into the evening, which can interfere with their sleep patterns. The blue light emitted by screens can suppress the production of melatonin, a hormone that regulates sleep, making it harder for children to fall asleep and stay asleep. Lack of sleep can have a profound impact on emotional regulation, as tired children are more likely to be irritable, anxious, and prone to mood swings. In the long term, chronic sleep deprivation can contribute to more serious emotional and mental health issues, such as depression and anxiety.

Technology also poses challenges to developing healthy social skills. Children who spend excessive time on screens may miss out on opportunities to practice important social skills, such as active listening, turn-taking, and reading social cues. These skills are typically developed through face-to-face interactions, where children learn to navigate the complexities of real-life relationships. For example, when children play together in person, they learn how to negotiate, share, and resolve conflicts. However, when most of their interactions take place online, they may not have the same opportunities to develop these essential social skills. As a result, children who rely heavily on digital communication may struggle with interpersonal relationships, both in childhood and later in life.

On the other hand, it's important to acknowledge that technology can also have positive effects on emotional development when used mindfully and in moderation. Educational apps, online therapy tools, and mental health resources can provide valuable support for children struggling with emotional challenges. For example, mindfulness apps designed for children can help them learn emotional regulation techniques such as deep breathing and meditation. Similarly, online communities can offer a sense of connection and belonging for children who may feel isolated or misunderstood in their offline lives. The key is to strike a balance between using technology for its benefits and ensuring that it does not interfere with emotional growth and face-to-face relationships.

Setting Healthy Boundaries in a Screen-Filled World

Given the pervasive presence of technology in modern life, setting healthy boundaries around screen time is essential for promoting emotional well-being and fostering healthy emotional development in children. Healthy boundaries help ensure that children's use of technology is balanced with other important aspects of life, such as physical activity, face-to-face interactions, and opportunities for emotional reflection. While it can be challenging to limit screen time in a world where technology is ubiquitous, there are several strategies that parents, educators, and caregivers can use to help children develop a balanced relationship with screens.

The first step in setting healthy boundaries is to establish clear guidelines for screen time. The American Academy of Pediatrics (AAP) recommends that children aged 2 to 5 have no more than one hour of screen time per day, while older children and adolescents should have consistent limits that prioritize sleep, physical activity, and other essential activities. It's important for parents to communicate these guidelines clearly to their children and to explain the reasons behind them. For example, parents might explain that too much screen time can make it harder to sleep, affect mood, or take time away from other fun and important activities like playing outside or spending time with family.

In addition to setting time limits, it's important to create screen-free zones and screen-free times. For example, the dinner table can be designated as a screen-free zone, where family members focus on conversation and connection rather than their devices. Similarly, parents can establish screen-free times, such as during meals, before bedtime, or during family activities. These boundaries help create a balance between screen time and other important aspects of family life, such as communication, relaxation, and bonding. For example, by making the hour before bedtime a screen-free time, parents can help their children wind down and prepare for a good night's sleep.

Another important strategy is to model healthy screen use. Children are more likely to follow screen time rules if they see their parents and caregivers practicing what they preach. If parents are constantly checking their phones or using devices during family time, children may struggle to understand why they are being asked to limit their own screen time. Modeling healthy habits—such as putting devices away during meals, taking breaks from screens to engage in physical activity, and prioritizing face-to-face interactions—shows children that technology is just one part of life, not the center of it. For example, parents can model healthy screen use by setting their own limits, such as avoiding social media in the evening or turning off notifications during family time.

Encouraging alternative activities is another effective way to set healthy boundaries around screen time. When children have access to engaging, non-screen activities, they are less likely to turn to technology out of boredom. Parents and educators can encourage activities such as outdoor play, reading, arts and crafts, sports, and imaginative play, all of which help support emotional development and social skills. For example, a child who enjoys playing video games might also be encouraged to join a local sports team or participate in a creative hobby like drawing or building with Legos. These activities not only provide a break from screens but also help children develop important life skills such as teamwork, problem-solving, and emotional regulation.

In addition to offering alternative activities, it's important to teach children self-regulation when it comes to screen time. Rather than simply enforcing strict rules, parents can help children develop the skills they need to manage their own screen use responsibly. For example, parents can talk to their children about the importance of taking breaks, setting limits, and being mindful of how screen time affects their mood and behavior. One way to promote self-regulation is to use a screen time tracker or app that allows children to monitor their own screen use and set goals for reducing time spent on screens. By involving children in the process of managing their screen time, parents can empower them to take ownership of their habits and develop self-discipline around technology use. This can be more effective in the long run than imposing external limits alone, as it teaches children how to make healthy choices for themselves. For example, a child might use a screen time tracker to observe that they spent four hours on video games over the weekend, and with guidance, they might set a goal to reduce that time to two hours and spend the extra time engaging in outdoor activities or hobbies.

Incorporating breaks and balance is another critical component of setting healthy screen boundaries. One method that can be introduced is the 20-20-20 rule: every 20 minutes of screen time should be followed by a 20-second break, during which the child looks at something 20 feet away. This practice helps reduce eye strain and encourages children to pause and step away from their devices regularly. Additionally, teachers and parents can encourage children to balance their screen time with activities that promote physical and emotional well-being, such as spending time outdoors, exercising, or engaging in creative activities like drawing or playing music.

It's also important to encourage mindful use of technology by helping children think critically about how they spend their time online and what content they are consuming. Mindfulness around technology involves being aware of how certain apps, games, or social media platforms affect emotions and behaviors. For example, children can be taught to reflect on how they feel after spending time on a particular platform—whether it makes them feel happy, relaxed, anxious, or frustrated—and adjust their usage accordingly. If a child notices that a social media app makes them feel stressed or left out, they can be encouraged to take a break from the app or limit their time on it.

Parents can also guide children toward positive and educational uses of technology. Rather than simply focusing on limiting screen time, it's valuable to direct children toward apps, games, and websites that support learning, creativity, and emotional development. For example, educational apps that teach problem-solving, coding, or art can provide enriching experiences that complement a child's screen time. Similarly, mindfulness apps designed for children can help them learn emotional regulation techniques such as deep breathing, meditation, and guided reflection.

Another critical aspect of managing screen time in a healthy way is addressing the issue of cyberbully and online safety. With increased screen time comes greater exposure to online risks, including cyberbully, inappropriate content, and social media pressures. Parents and educators must take proactive steps to teach children about online safety, privacy, and the importance of setting boundaries in their digital interactions. Children should be taught to recognize signs of cyberbully, know how to report harmful behavior, and understand the importance of protecting their personal information online. For example, parents can have regular conversations with their children about their online activities, checking in to ensure that they feel safe and supported in their digital environments.

In terms of setting consequences for overuse, it's important for parents to establish clear and consistent rules regarding screen time and to enforce those rules with appropriate consequences when necessary. For example, if a child consistently exceeds their allotted screen time or uses technology inappropriately, parents might reduce their access to devices or require them to take a longer break from screens. However, it's equally important that consequences are applied in a way that is supportive rather than punitive. Rather than simply taking away devices, parents can use these moments as opportunities to discuss the importance of balance and to help the child reflect on their screen habits and emotional responses.

In some cases, parents and educators may need to address screen time as a family issue rather than placing the burden solely on the child. Often, children's screen habits mirror those of the adults around them. If parents are constantly checking their phones or working on their laptops during family time, it becomes more difficult for children to understand why they should limit their own screen use. Families can work together to create shared screen time rules, such as designating certain hours of the day as screen-free or committing to technology-free family activities. By approaching screen time as a family issue, parents can model healthy behaviors and create a more balanced and emotionally supportive environment for everyone.

For educators, managing screen time in the classroom involves setting clear expectations for when and how technology is used during the school day. While technology can be a valuable tool for learning, it's important that it doesn't dominate the educational experience. Teachers can incorporate screen breaks into the school day, encouraging students to step away from their devices and engage in hands-on activities, physical movement, or face-to-face interactions with their peers. Teachers can also use technology in the classroom in ways that promote collaboration and creativity, such as assigning group projects that require students to work together in person while using technology as a supplementary tool.

Finally, it's important to recognize that flexibility is key when setting screen time boundaries. Every child is different, and what works for one family may not work for another. Some children may have greater difficulty regulating their screen use due to personality differences, attention challenges, or emotional needs, and these factors should be taken into account when setting limits. The goal is not to eliminate technology altogether but to help children develop a balanced and mindful approach to their screen time. Parents and educators should remain open to adjusting boundaries as needed, based on the child's emotional and social development, and should focus on fostering a positive relationship with technology that supports overall well-being.

In conclusion, managing screen time and emotions in the digital age requires a thoughtful and proactive approach. Technology has a profound impact on emotional development, from how children interact with others to how they process their own feelings. By setting healthy boundaries, encouraging mindful and balanced use of screens, and teaching children the skills they need to navigate the digital world, parents and educators can help ensure that technology supports, rather than undermines, emotional intelligence and well-being. Through these efforts, children can learn to enjoy the benefits of technology while maintaining the emotional and social connections that are so vital for their development.

Fostering Resilience in Children

Teaching Kids How to Bounce Back from Setbacks

Resilience is a fundamental aspect of emotional intelligence, enabling children to cope with adversity, adapt to challenges, and ultimately thrive even in difficult circumstances. Resilience is not an inherent trait but a skill that can be cultivated and developed over time, particularly through childhood and adolescence. In an ever-changing world filled with uncertainties, teaching children how to bounce back from setbacks is critical to their emotional and psychological well-being. By developing resilience, children gain the ability to face life's inevitable challenges, whether they are related to academic difficulties, social conflicts, or personal disappointments.

One of the most effective ways to foster resilience in children is by helping them re-frame setbacks as opportunities for growth. Setbacks can trigger a range of emotions, including frustration, sadness, anger, or disappointment. Children may feel discouraged and may begin to believe that they are incapable of overcoming challenges. However, when children are taught to view setbacks as learning experiences, they can develop a growth mindset—a belief that their abilities and intelligence can be developed through effort and persistence. For example, a child who struggles with a math test might initially feel discouraged, but with the guidance of a caregiver or teacher, they can be encouraged to see the experience as an opportunity to improve their skills. Instead of focusing on failure, the child learns to focus on what they can do differently next time, such as studying more effectively or seeking additional help.

To help children re-frame setbacks, parents and educators can encourage reflective thinking. After a difficult experience, it's important to guide children through a reflection process that allows them to identify what went wrong, what they learned, and how they can apply that knowledge to future situations. For instance, after losing a soccer game, a parent might ask their child, "What did you think you did well in the game? What would you like to work on for next time?" This type of questioning helps children focus on both their strengths and areas for improvement, fostering resilience by reinforcing the idea that setbacks are a normal part of the learning process.

Another key aspect of fostering resilience is teaching children problem-solving skills. When children encounter setbacks, they need to develop the ability to assess the situation and come up with potential solutions. Instead of allowing feelings of helplessness or defeat to take over, resilient children are equipped with the skills to tackle the problem head-on. For example, if a child is struggling with a group project at school because they feel their ideas aren't being heard, a parent or teacher can help the child brainstorm strategies for addressing the issue, such as speaking up during group discussions, asking the teacher for guidance, or finding a way to compromise with their peers. By teaching children how to approach challenges with a solution-focused mindset, adults can help them build confidence in their ability to navigate difficulties.

Emotional regulation is another essential component of resilience. Children who are able to manage their emotions in the face of setbacks are more likely to persevere through challenges rather than becoming overwhelmed or giving up. Teaching emotional regulation involves helping children recognize their emotions, understand what triggers them, and develop strategies for managing them in a healthy way. For example, when a child becomes frustrated with a difficult homework assignment, a caregiver might teach them deep breathing techniques or encourage them to take a short break before returning to the task. Over time, these strategies become internalized, allowing children to regulate their emotions more effectively and maintain a sense of control when faced with adversity.

In addition to emotional regulation, fostering resilience also involves developing a strong support system. Resilient children often have supportive relationships with family members, teachers, friends, and mentors who provide encouragement and guidance during tough times. These relationships offer children a sense of security and belonging, which helps them feel more confident in their ability to overcome challenges. For example, a child who is dealing with the loss of a pet may find comfort in talking to their parents about their feelings or seeking reassurance from a close friend. Knowing that they have a network of people who care about them can make it easier for children to face difficult emotions and bounce back from setbacks.

Parents and educators can also help children build resilience by setting realistic expectations and encouraging perseverance. While it's important to challenge children and encourage them to strive for their best, it's equally important to ensure that expectations are achievable and aligned with the child's developmental stage and abilities. Unrealistic expectations can lead to feelings of failure and inadequacy, which may erode resilience. For example, if a child is struggling with a particular subject in school, it may be more helpful to set smaller, incremental goals (such as improving a specific skill) rather than expecting immediate mastery. By breaking down larger challenges into smaller, more manageable steps, children learn that progress is possible even in the face of setbacks.

At the same time, encouraging perseverance and grit teaches children that persistence is key to overcoming obstacles. Instead of allowing children to give up when they encounter difficulty, parents and teachers can encourage them to keep trying and to see failure as a temporary setback rather than a permanent roadblock. This can be done through positive reinforcement, such as praising a child for their effort and determination even if the outcome isn't perfect. For example, after a child struggles with a difficult puzzle, a parent might say, "I'm really proud of how hard you worked on that. You didn't give up, and that's what matters most." This reinforces the idea that resilience comes from effort and persistence, not just from success.

Building a sense of purpose is another powerful way to foster resilience. When children have a clear sense of purpose—whether it's related to their academics, hobbies, or relationships—they are more likely to stay motivated and focused, even in the face of setbacks. For example, a child who is passionate about learning to play the piano may be more resilient when they encounter challenges, such as struggling with a difficult piece of music, because they are driven by their love of music and their desire to improve. Encouraging children to explore their interests, set meaningful goals, and find purpose in their activities can help them develop the resilience they need to overcome obstacles.

Finally, fostering resilience in children involves teaching them the importance of self-compassion. Resilient children understand that everyone makes mistakes and experiences setbacks, and they learn to treat themselves with kindness and understanding when things don't go as planned. Instead of being overly critical of themselves, resilient children are able to acknowledge their mistakes, learn from them, and move forward without dwelling on feelings of failure. Parents and educators can model self-compassion by demonstrating forgiveness and understanding when children make mistakes and by encouraging children to speak to themselves in a kind and supportive way. For example, if a child feels bad about making a mistake during a class presentation, a teacher might remind them, "It's okay to make mistakes—we all do. What's important is that you tried your best, and you can learn from this for next time."

Building Confidence Through Emotional Awareness

Confidence is closely tied to emotional intelligence, as children who are emotionally aware are better equipped to understand their strengths and challenges, regulate their emotions, and approach new experiences with a sense of self-assurance. Emotional awareness involves recognizing and understanding one's own emotions as well as the emotions of others. By helping children develop emotional awareness, parents and educators can build their confidence and empower them to navigate life's challenges with greater ease and resilience.

Self-awareness is the foundation of emotional awareness and is essential for building confidence. Children who are self-aware are able to recognize their emotions as they arise, understand why they are feeling a certain way, and identify how their emotions influence their thoughts and behaviors. For example, a child who is nervous before giving a speech in class might be able to identify that their nervousness comes from fear of being judged by their peers. This awareness allows the child to take proactive steps to manage their anxiety, such as practicing deep breathing or reminding themselves that it's okay to make mistakes.

Building self-awareness in children starts with teaching them to label their emotions. Often, children may feel overwhelmed by emotions that they don't fully understand, which can lead to feelings of confusion or helplessness. By giving children the vocabulary to describe their emotions—such as happy, sad, frustrated, or excited—parents and educators help them make sense of their feelings. For example, when a child says, "I feel angry," a parent might respond by asking, "What do you think is making you feel that way?" This encourages the child to reflect on the cause of their emotions, which is the first step toward managing those feelings.

Once children are able to identify their emotions, the next step is teaching them how to express their emotions in a healthy way. Confidence grows when children feel that they are able to communicate their emotions effectively and that their feelings are valued and respected by the people around them. Parents and educators can encourage emotional expression by creating a safe space where children feel comfortable sharing their feelings without fear of judgment or punishment. For example, if a child is upset because they had a fight with a friend, a parent might say, "It sounds like you're feeling really hurt right now. Let's talk about what happened." This type of response validates the child's emotions and shows them that it's okay to talk about their feelings.

In addition to helping children express their emotions, emotional awareness involves teaching them how to regulate their emotions. Confidence is built when children know that they have the tools to manage their emotions, even in stressful or challenging situations. Emotional regulation skills, such as deep breathing, mindfulness, or taking a break, give children a sense of control over their emotional experiences. For example, a child who is feeling anxious before a big test might practice taking slow, deep breaths to calm their nerves. By teaching children these coping strategies, parents and educators empower them to face difficult emotions with confidence.

Another important aspect of building confidence through emotional awareness is teaching empathy and helping children understand the emotions of others. Empathy is the ability to recognize, understand, and share the feelings of another person. When children develop empathy, they become more adept at navigating social interactions, building meaningful relationships, and resolving conflicts. Empathy also helps children feel more connected to those around them, which can boost their confidence in social settings. For instance, when a child can empathize with a friend who is feeling sad, they may feel more capable of offering support and comfort, which strengthens their social bonds and self-esteem.

Teaching empathy starts with modeling empathetic behavior. Parents and educators can demonstrate empathy by showing understanding and concern for others' emotions, whether it's by listening actively, offering help, or expressing compassion in difficult situations. For example, if a child is upset because they were excluded from a game at recess, a teacher might say, "That must have been really hard for you. I'm sorry that happened—let's think about what we can do next time." By modeling empathy, adults teach children how to respond to the emotions of others in a caring and thoughtful way.

Additionally, role-playing activities can be an effective way to teach empathy. Children can act out different scenarios in which they are encouraged to consider how another person might be feeling and how they might respond in a supportive manner. For example, a role-playing activity might involve one child pretending to be upset about losing a toy, while another child practices offering comfort by saying, "I'm sorry you're upset. Would you like to play with something else?" These activities help children practice empathy in a safe and structured environment, allowing them to develop the social and emotional skills necessary to build positive relationships.

Positive self-talk is another tool that helps build confidence through emotional awareness. Many children, especially those who struggle with setbacks, may develop negative thought patterns, such as telling themselves, "I'm not good enough" or "I'll never be able to do this." These negative thoughts can erode a child's confidence and make it harder for them to bounce back from challenges. Teaching children to replace negative self-talk with positive affirmations, such as "I can try again" or "I'm proud of how hard I'm working," helps them develop a more optimistic mindset. For example, when a child is feeling nervous about performing in a school play, a parent might encourage them to say, "I've practiced a lot, and I'm ready to do my best." This shift in thinking helps children approach challenges with greater confidence and resilience.

In addition to fostering a positive internal dialogue, building confidence also involves acknowledging and celebrating emotional growth. When children successfully manage their emotions, whether it's staying calm during a stressful situation or expressing their feelings in a constructive way, it's important for parents and educators to recognize and celebrate those achievements. This positive reinforcement helps children feel proud of their emotional progress and encourages them to continue developing their emotional intelligence. For example, after a child handles a difficult conversation with a friend, a parent might say, "I'm really impressed by how you expressed your feelings so calmly. That shows a lot of emotional strength." By celebrating emotional milestones, adults help children build a sense of pride and confidence in their ability to manage their emotions effectively.

Encouraging independence and responsibility also plays a significant role in building confidence through emotional awareness. When children are given opportunities to make their own decisions and take responsibility for their actions, they develop a sense of autonomy and self-efficacy. For instance, allowing children to choose how they want to handle a conflict with a sibling, rather than solving the problem for them, helps them develop problem-solving skills and confidence in their ability to navigate social and emotional challenges. Parents and educators can support this process by offering guidance and suggestions, but ultimately allowing the child to take ownership of the situation. This not only builds emotional resilience but also fosters a sense of competence and self-reliance.

Finally, providing a supportive and nurturing environment is essential for fostering confidence and emotional awareness in children. Children are more likely to feel confident and emotionally secure when they know they are supported by the adults in their lives. This support comes in many forms, such as offering encouragement during difficult times, providing a safe space to express emotions, and being available to listen and offer guidance when needed. For example, a child who feels overwhelmed by schoolwork might benefit from a parent who says, "I know this is hard right now, but I'm here to help you, and we can work through it together." Knowing that they have a supportive network gives children the confidence to take risks, try new things, and face challenges head-on.

In conclusion, building confidence through emotional awareness involves teaching children to recognize and understand their emotions, develop empathy for others, regulate their emotions effectively, and engage in positive self-talk. By fostering emotional awareness, parents and educators empower children to navigate life's challenges with resilience, confidence, and a strong sense of self. With these skills, children are better equipped to bounce back from setbacks, build meaningful relationships, and approach new experiences with a sense of curiosity and self-assurance.

Emotional Intelligence and Academic Success

The Link Between Emotional Intelligence and School Performance

Emotional intelligence (EI) is increasingly recognized as a key factor in academic success. While traditional markers of academic achievement—such as IQ and cognitive skills—remain important, research has shown that emotional intelligence significantly contributes to students' performance in school. EI encompasses the ability to recognize, understand, manage, and express emotions in a healthy way, as well as the capacity to empathize with others and build positive social relationships. These skills play a critical role in how students navigate the academic environment, manage stress, approach challenges, and collaborate with peers.

One of the most direct links between emotional intelligence and academic success is emotional regulation, which refers to the ability to manage and respond to emotions in a constructive manner. In the context of school, students often experience a range of emotions, including anxiety, frustration, excitement, and disappointment. Those with high emotional intelligence are better equipped to regulate these emotions, allowing them to maintain focus and motivation even in the face of challenges. For example, a student who feels anxious before a test may use emotional regulation strategies—such as deep breathing, positive self-talk, or mindfulness—to calm their nerves and perform to the best of their ability. In contrast, a student who struggles with emotional regulation may become overwhelmed by anxiety, leading to impaired concentration, poor performance, or avoidance of academic tasks altogether.

Emotional regulation also helps students persevere through difficult assignments or subjects. Rather than giving up when faced with a challenging math problem or a complicated essay, emotionally intelligent students are more likely to approach the task with resilience and a problem-solving mindset. They understand that frustration is a natural part of the learning process and that emotions such as impatience or discouragement can be managed. This ability to stay calm and composed in the face of academic challenges directly contributes to better outcomes, as it allows students to keep working toward their goals without being derailed by negative emotions.

Another crucial component of emotional intelligence that impacts academic success is self-awareness. Self-awareness is the ability to recognize and understand one's own emotions, strengths, weaknesses, and motivations. In the academic setting, self-awareness allows students to take responsibility for their learning and make informed decisions about how to improve. For instance, a student who is aware that they struggle with time management might develop strategies to stay organized, such as creating a study schedule or setting reminders for upcoming assignments. Similarly, a student who recognizes that they feel anxious before presentations might practice public speaking in advance to build confidence.

Self-awareness also plays a key role in goal setting and motivation. Emotionally intelligent students are more likely to set realistic and achievable academic goals, which helps them stay motivated and focused on their studies. They are able to reflect on their progress and adjust their goals as needed, rather than becoming discouraged by setbacks. For example, a student who struggles with a science project might set smaller, incremental goals—such as completing one section of the project each day—rather than feeling overwhelmed by the entire task. This ability to break down larger tasks into manageable steps is a hallmark of both emotional intelligence and academic success, as it helps students stay engaged and productive.

Empathy, another key aspect of emotional intelligence, also plays an important role in academic success, particularly in collaborative learning environments. Empathy allows students to understand and appreciate the perspectives of their peers, which is essential for group projects, discussions, and classroom dynamics. When students are able to empathize with others, they are more likely to engage in positive social behaviors, such as active listening, cooperation, and conflict resolution. For example, in a group project, an empathetic student might recognize that one of their peers is feeling overwhelmed and offer support or help divide the work more equitably. These social skills not only enhance the learning experience but also contribute to a positive and inclusive classroom environment, which is conducive to academic achievement.

Furthermore, emotionally intelligent students tend to have stronger communication skills, which are critical for academic success. The ability to express thoughts and ideas clearly, both in writing and verbally, is essential in almost every academic discipline. Whether participating in class discussions, writing essays, or giving presentations, students with high emotional intelligence are better able to articulate their ideas, respond to feedback, and engage with their teachers and peers. Emotional intelligence also helps students handle constructive criticism effectively. Rather than becoming defensive or discouraged when receiving feedback on their work, emotionally intelligent students are able to view criticism as an opportunity for growth and improvement.

Emotional intelligence also influences how students handle academic stress and pressure. School can be a source of significant stress, particularly for students who are juggling multiple assignments, tests, extracurricular activities, and social responsibilities. Emotional intelligence provides students with the tools to manage this stress in healthy ways. For example, students who are able to recognize when they are feeling overwhelmed can take proactive steps to reduce their stress, such as practicing relaxation techniques, seeking support from a teacher or counselor, or organizing their time more effectively. This ability to manage stress not only improves academic performance but also contributes to better overall well-being.

In addition to helping students manage stress, emotional intelligence promotes emotional resilience, or the ability to bounce back from setbacks and failures. Academic life is filled with both successes and challenges, and emotionally intelligent students are more likely to view failures as opportunities for learning rather than as personal defeats. For example, a student who receives a lower grade than expected on a test might initially feel disappointed, but with emotional resilience, they can reflect on what went wrong, seek help if needed, and use the experience to improve on future assessments. This capacity to recover from academic setbacks is a crucial factor in long-term success, as it prevents students from becoming discouraged and disengaged from their studies.

Finally, emotional intelligence contributes to academic engagement and motivation by fostering a positive attitude toward learning. Students who are emotionally intelligent are more likely to be curious, open to new ideas, and intrinsically motivated to learn. They see learning as a process of growth and self-improvement, rather than as a series of tasks to be completed for external validation. This love for learning is closely tied to emotional intelligence, as it involves the ability to regulate emotions like frustration and boredom, empathize with different perspectives, and take pride in personal progress.

Encouraging a Love for Learning Through Emotional Skills

Developing a love for learning is one of the most important goals of education, and emotional intelligence plays a vital role in fostering this intrinsic motivation. Children who are emotionally intelligent are more likely to approach learning with enthusiasm, curiosity, and a willingness to embrace challenges. By nurturing emotional skills in students, parents and educators can help cultivate a lifelong passion for learning that extends beyond academic achievements.

One of the key ways to encourage a love for learning is by promoting a growth mindset, which is the belief that intelligence and abilities can be developed through effort, practice, and persistence. A growth mindset is closely linked to emotional intelligence, as it requires the ability to regulate emotions like frustration and disappointment when faced with challenges. Children with a growth mindset view mistakes as opportunities to learn rather than as indicators of failure. For example, when a student struggles with a difficult math problem, they might initially feel frustrated, but with the encouragement of a teacher who emphasizes effort and perseverance, they can learn to view the challenge as an opportunity to improve their skills.

Educators and parents can foster a growth mindset by celebrating effort and progress, rather than focusing solely on outcomes. Instead of praising a child only for getting the right answer or achieving a high grade, it's important to acknowledge the hard work and persistence that led to their success. For example, a teacher might say, "I'm really proud of how hard you worked on this project. You didn't give up, even when it was difficult, and that's what helped you succeed." This type of feedback reinforces the idea that learning is a process and that effort is more important than perfection. When children feel that their hard work is valued, they are more likely to stay motivated and engaged in their learning.

Curiosity is another key factor in developing a love for learning, and emotional intelligence plays a role in fostering curiosity by helping children manage the uncertainty and discomfort that often come with exploring new ideas. Curiosity requires an openness to new experiences and a willingness to ask questions, even when the answers are not immediately clear. Emotionally intelligent children are better able to tolerate ambiguity and approach new challenges with curiosity rather than fear. For example, a student who is curious about how plants grow might ask their teacher questions, conduct experiments, and explore different sources of information, even if they don't fully understand the answers right away. This willingness to explore and experiment is a hallmark of a love for learning, and it's supported by emotional intelligence skills such as resilience, patience, and self-regulation.

Intrinsic motivation, or the desire to learn for the sake of learning itself, is also closely tied to emotional intelligence. Intrinsic motivation comes from within, driven by a genuine interest in a subject or a desire for personal growth, rather than by external rewards such as grades or praise. Emotionally intelligent students are more likely to be intrinsically motivated because they are able to regulate their emotions and find satisfaction in the learning process itself. For example, a child who enjoys solving puzzles might spend hours working on complex problems, not because they want to win a prize, but because they find the challenge engaging and rewarding. This intrinsic motivation leads to deeper learning and a more sustained interest in academic subjects.

Parents and educators can encourage intrinsic motivation by creating a supportive and stimulating learning environment. This involves providing students with opportunities to explore their interests, ask questions, and take ownership of their learning. For example, teachers can offer students choices in how they complete assignments or allow them to pursue independent projects on topics that interest them. By giving students a sense of autonomy and control over their learning, educators help them develop a love for learning that is driven by their own curiosity and passions.

In addition to fostering intrinsic motivation, emotional intelligence helps children develop a sense of purpose in their learning. A sense of purpose gives students a clear understanding of why their learning matters and how it connects to their personal goals, values, and the world around them. When students see the relevance of what they are learning, they are more likely to stay engaged and motivated. Emotional intelligence plays a key role in developing this sense of purpose, as it helps students reflect on their interests, passions, and long-term goals.

For example, a student who is passionate about environmental issues might find purpose in studying science because they want to contribute to solutions for climate change. When students are emotionally aware and able to connect their learning to something meaningful, they are more likely to approach schoolwork with enthusiasm and dedication. Teachers and parents can encourage this by helping students see the real-world applications of what they are learning. For instance, a teacher might explain how math skills are used in architecture or how writing skills are essential for advocacy work. By helping students make these connections, educators can foster a love for learning that is rooted in a deeper understanding of its purpose.

Resilience is another emotional skill that supports a love for learning. Learning is a process that inevitably involves setbacks, mistakes, and challenges, and emotionally intelligent students are better equipped to handle these difficulties without becoming discouraged. Resilience enables students to persevere in the face of academic challenges and to view obstacles as opportunities for growth rather than as insurmountable barriers. For example, a student who fails a test may feel disappointed, but with resilience, they can bounce back by reviewing their mistakes, seeking help from a teacher, and preparing more effectively for the next test. This resilience not only helps students succeed academically but also fosters a positive attitude toward learning.

Parents and educators can promote resilience by normalizing failure and emphasizing the importance of perseverance. Children need to understand that failure is a natural part of the learning process and that it's okay to make mistakes as long as they continue to put in effort and learn from their experiences. For instance, a teacher might share stories of famous inventors or scientists who failed multiple times before achieving success, reinforcing the message that perseverance is key to achieving one's goals. By creating a classroom culture that celebrates effort and resilience, educators help students develop the confidence and determination they need to keep learning, even when things get tough.

Another way to encourage a love for learning through emotional skills is by teaching students self-regulation strategies that help them stay focused and manage distractions. In today's world, students are constantly bombarded with distractions, from smartphones and social media to extracurricular activities and peer pressure. Emotional intelligence equips students with the skills they need to manage these distractions and stay on task. For example, a student who is easily distracted during homework time might practice mindfulness techniques, such as deep breathing or setting specific time blocks for focused work, to help them stay on track. By teaching students how to regulate their emotions and attention, parents and educators help them develop the self-discipline needed for academic success and a sustained love for learning.

Growth mindset language is another powerful tool for fostering a love for learning through emotional skills. When parents and educators use language that emphasizes growth, effort, and the potential for improvement, they help children develop a positive attitude toward learning. For example, instead of saying, "You're so smart," which focuses on innate ability, a teacher might say, "I can see how hard you worked on this, and your effort really paid off." This type of feedback encourages children to view learning as a process of growth and development, rather than as a fixed measure of ability. By reinforcing the idea that learning is about progress, not perfection, parents and teachers help children approach challenges with confidence and curiosity.

Collaborative learning also benefits from emotional intelligence. Working in groups or with peers requires students to navigate complex social interactions, manage conflicts, and communicate effectively. Emotionally intelligent students are more likely to thrive in these collaborative environments because they are able to empathize with others, listen actively, and contribute to group problem-solving. For instance, in a group science project, a student with strong emotional intelligence might help mediate a disagreement between group members, ensuring that everyone's ideas are heard and valued. This collaborative spirit not only enhances academic outcomes but also fosters a love for learning by making the process of discovery and problem-solving more engaging and enjoyable.

Finally, emotional intelligence helps students develop positive relationships with their teachers, which is crucial for academic success and a love for learning. When students feel emotionally connected to their teachers, they are more likely to feel supported, motivated, and engaged in the learning process. Teachers who demonstrate empathy, understanding, and emotional support create a classroom environment where students feel safe to take risks, ask questions, and explore new ideas. This positive teacher-student relationship can have a profound impact on a child's attitude toward learning. For example, a student who feels understood and supported by their teacher is more likely to seek help when needed and to stay motivated even when the material becomes challenging.

In conclusion, the link between emotional intelligence and academic success is undeniable. Emotional skills such as self-awareness, emotional regulation, empathy, resilience, and positive communication not only contribute to better academic outcomes but also foster a genuine love for learning. By teaching and nurturing emotional intelligence in students, parents and educators can help children develop the confidence, curiosity, and motivation they need to succeed both in school and in life. Through emotional intelligence, students learn to approach challenges with a growth mindset, build meaningful relationships, and find joy in the process of learning itself.

Preparing Children for Future Challenges

The Long-term Benefits of Emotional Intelligence in Adulthood

Emotional intelligence (EI) is not only crucial during childhood and adolescence but also has long-lasting benefits that extend well into adulthood. As children grow, they face increasingly complex social, academic, and professional challenges, and those who possess strong emotional intelligence skills are better equipped to navigate these difficulties with resilience, confidence, and emotional stability. By fostering emotional intelligence early on, parents and educators can set children on a path toward success in their personal relationships, careers, and overall well-being.

One of the most significant long-term benefits of emotional intelligence is its impact on interpersonal relationships. Emotionally intelligent adults are better able to form and maintain healthy, meaningful relationships, both in their personal lives and in the workplace. The ability to empathize with others, understand social dynamics, and communicate effectively are all rooted in emotional intelligence. For example, adults who have developed strong empathy skills during childhood are more likely to engage in supportive and collaborative relationships with their partners, friends, and colleagues. This ability to connect with others on an emotional level not only strengthens social bonds but also contributes to greater personal satisfaction and fulfillment.

Emotional intelligence also plays a key role in conflict resolution and problem-solving. Adults with high emotional intelligence are more likely to approach conflicts with a calm, solution-focused mindset, rather than reacting impulsively or defensively. They are able to manage their own emotions during difficult situations and are more likely to listen actively to the perspectives of others, which facilitates constructive dialogue and compromise. For example, in a workplace dispute, an emotionally intelligent individual might calmly express their concerns while also considering the needs and emotions of their colleagues, leading to a resolution that benefits everyone involved. This ability to navigate conflicts effectively is essential for success in both personal and professional settings, as it helps individuals maintain positive relationships and avoid unnecessary tension.

In addition to improving interpersonal relationships, emotional intelligence contributes to career success and leadership potential. In today's fast-paced and competitive work environment, technical skills alone are not enough to ensure success. Employers increasingly value emotional intelligence, as it enables employees to collaborate effectively, manage stress, and adapt to changing circumstances. For example, a manager who can recognize and regulate their own emotions, as well as those of their team members, is better equipped to motivate and support their team, leading to higher productivity and job satisfaction. Similarly, emotionally intelligent leaders are more likely to inspire trust and loyalty among their colleagues, as they are able to demonstrate empathy, integrity, and emotional stability in their decision-making.

Moreover, emotional intelligence is closely linked to emotional resilience, which is critical for handling the inevitable challenges and setbacks that arise in adulthood. Life is full of stressors, from career disappointments to personal losses, and those with high emotional intelligence are better able to cope with these difficulties without becoming overwhelmed. Emotional resilience allows individuals to bounce back from adversity, learn from their experiences, and continue moving forward with a positive mindset. For example, an adult who loses their job might initially feel discouraged, but with emotional resilience, they can process their emotions in a healthy way, seek support from their social network, and take proactive steps to find new opportunities. This ability to adapt and persevere through life's challenges is essential for long-term success and well-being.

Emotional regulation is another long-term benefit of emotional intelligence that significantly impacts adulthood. The ability to manage emotions effectively helps adults navigate high-pressure situations with composure and clarity. For example, an emotionally intelligent adult who faces a stressful deadline at work might recognize their feelings of anxiety and use coping strategies, such as time management techniques, deep breathing, or prioritization, to stay focused and calm. Emotional regulation also helps adults avoid impulsive decisions that are driven by short-term emotions, leading to better decision-making in both personal and professional contexts.

Furthermore, emotional intelligence contributes to mental health and overall well-being. Adults who have strong emotional intelligence are more likely to experience positive mental health outcomes, as they are better equipped to handle stress, regulate their emotions, and maintain supportive relationships. For example, emotionally intelligent individuals are less likely to engage in harmful coping mechanisms, such as substance abuse or emotional withdrawal, when faced with challenges. Instead, they are more likely to seek healthy outlets for managing their emotions, such as talking to a trusted friend, practicing mindfulness, or engaging in physical activity. This proactive approach to mental health helps reduce the risk of anxiety, depression, and other emotional difficulties, leading to greater overall life satisfaction.

Self-awareness, another key component of emotional intelligence, also plays a vital role in adulthood. Adults who are self-aware are better able to recognize their strengths, weaknesses, and emotional triggers, which allows them to make more informed decisions about their personal and professional lives. For example, a self-aware adult might recognize that they thrive in collaborative work environments and therefore seek out job opportunities that align with their interpersonal strengths. Similarly, self-awareness helps individuals identify areas for personal growth and development, enabling them to pursue opportunities for continuous self-improvement. This ability to reflect on one's emotions and behaviors is essential for achieving long-term personal and professional success.

Finally, emotional intelligence fosters a growth mindset, which is the belief that abilities and intelligence can be developed through effort and perseverance. Adults with a growth mindset are more likely to embrace challenges, view setbacks as opportunities for learning, and persist in the face of obstacles. This mindset is closely linked to emotional intelligence, as it requires the ability to regulate emotions such as frustration and self-doubt, as well as the resilience to keep trying even when success is not immediate. For example, an entrepreneur who faces multiple business failures might continue to iterate on their ideas and seek out new strategies, driven by the belief that they can improve and succeed through hard work and persistence. This growth mindset not only leads to greater personal and professional achievement but also promotes lifelong learning and adaptability.

Helping Children Transition to Adolescence and Beyond

As children grow and transition into adolescence, they face a host of new emotional, social, and academic challenges. Adolescence is a critical period of development, marked by significant changes in identity, relationships, and emotional regulation. During this time, emotional intelligence becomes even more important, as it helps adolescents navigate the complexities of their evolving emotional landscape and prepares them for the challenges of young adulthood.

One of the key challenges adolescents face is identity formation. Adolescence is a time when young people begin to explore who they are, what they believe in, and how they fit into the world around them. This process of identity formation can be emotionally turbulent, as adolescents may experience confusion, self-doubt, and conflicting emotions. Emotional intelligence helps adolescents navigate this process by promoting self-awareness and emotional regulation. For example, a teenager who is struggling with feelings of self-doubt might use emotional regulation strategies, such as journalism or talking to a trusted adult, to process their emotions in a healthy way. By developing emotional intelligence, adolescents are better able to understand and manage the complex emotions that arise during this critical period of self-discovery.

In addition to identity formation, peer relationships become increasingly important during adolescence. Friendships and social connections play a central role in adolescents' emotional and social development, and emotionally intelligent teens are more likely to form healthy, supportive relationships with their peers. Empathy, active listening, and conflict resolution are all essential skills for maintaining positive relationships, and these skills are rooted in emotional intelligence. For example, a teenager who notices that their friend is feeling left out during a group activity might offer support and include their friend in the conversation, demonstrating empathy and emotional awareness. By fostering emotional intelligence in adolescence, parents and educators can help young people build the social skills they need to form strong, lasting friendships.

At the same time, peer pressure and social comparison can pose significant challenges for adolescents. As teenagers become more aware of social dynamics and begin to compare themselves to their peers, they may experience feelings of inadequacy, anxiety, or pressure to conform. Emotional intelligence helps adolescents manage these challenges by promoting self-confidence and emotional resilience. For example, a teenager who feels pressured to fit in with a certain social group might use self-awareness to recognize that their values and interests are different from those of the group, and emotional regulation to resist the pressure to conform. By developing emotional intelligence, adolescents are better equipped to stay true to themselves and navigate the social pressures of adolescence with confidence.

Emotional regulation is particularly important during adolescence, as this is a time when emotions can feel especially intense and difficult to manage. Adolescents may experience heightened emotions such as anger, frustration, sadness, and excitement, and without the skills to regulate these emotions, they may engage in impulsive or risky behaviors. For example, an emotionally intelligent teenager who feels angry after an argument with a parent might take a few deep breaths or go for a walk to calm down, rather than lashing out in anger. By teaching adolescents emotional regulation strategies, parents and educators can help them manage their emotions in a healthy way, reducing the likelihood of emotional outbursts or harmful behaviors.

The transition to independence is another major challenge that adolescents face as they prepare to enter adulthood. During this time, young people begin to take on more responsibility for their own decisions, from managing their time and finances to making choices about their future education or career paths. Emotional intelligence is crucial for helping adolescents develop the self-discipline, decision-making skills, and resilience they need to navigate this transition successfully. For example, a teenager who is deciding which college to attend might use emotional intelligence to reflect on their goals, weigh the pros and cons of different options, and seek advice from trusted mentors. This ability to make thoughtful, informed decisions is a key component of emotional intelligence and is essential for navigating the challenges of young adulthood.

Finally, as adolescents transition to adulthood, they must learn to balance their personal and professional goals with their emotional well-being. Emotional intelligence helps young adults prioritize self-care and maintain a healthy work-life balance, even as they take on new responsibilities in their careers, relationships , and personal development. Emotionally intelligent young adults are more likely to recognize when they are feeling overwhelmed, stressed, or emotionally drained, and they have the tools to address these feelings in a healthy and constructive manner. For example, a young adult who is working long hours at a new job might notice signs of burnout—such as irritability, fatigue, or difficulty concentrating—and take proactive steps to address the issue, such as scheduling time for rest, engaging in physical activity, or seeking support from friends or a therapist. By developing emotional intelligence, adolescents can carry these skills into adulthood, allowing them to maintain their mental and emotional health while pursuing their personal and professional goals.

As adolescents grow into young adults, they also face challenges related to relationship building in both personal and professional contexts. Emotionally intelligent individuals are better equipped to navigate romantic relationships, friendships, and professional connections with maturity and respect. For instance, emotionally intelligent young adults understand the importance of clear communication, empathy, and mutual support in maintaining healthy relationships. In romantic relationships, for example, emotional intelligence helps individuals express their feelings openly, listen to their partner's concerns, and resolve conflicts constructively. This ability to manage emotions and build positive, supportive relationships sets the foundation for long-term relationship success in adulthood.

In the professional realm, emotional intelligence is increasingly recognized as a critical skill for career success and leadership. Employers value employees who are emotionally intelligent, as they are better able to collaborate with colleagues, manage workplace stress, and adapt to change. Young adults who have developed emotional intelligence are more likely to succeed in their careers, as they can navigate the social dynamics of the workplace, build positive relationships with their coworkers, and demonstrate leadership qualities. For example, an emotionally intelligent leader is able to motivate and inspire their team by understanding the emotional needs of their employees, offering support when needed, and creating a positive and inclusive work environment.

Moreover, emotional intelligence helps young adults handle rejection and setbacks with resilience and grace. Whether it's being turned down for a job, experiencing a breakup, or facing academic challenges, emotionally intelligent individuals are better equipped to process their emotions, learn from their experiences, and move forward with confidence. For instance, a young adult who doesn't get accepted into their dream college might initially feel disappointed, but with emotional intelligence, they can reflect on the situation, seek alternative paths, and maintain a positive outlook. This ability to recover from setbacks and maintain emotional stability is crucial for long-term success and well-being in adulthood.

Parents and educators can support adolescents in their journey toward emotional intelligence by providing guidance, encouragement, and opportunities for self-reflection. For example, they can create a safe space for adolescents to express their emotions and explore their identities without fear of judgment. This might involve having open conversations about the challenges of adolescence, offering support during difficult times, and encouraging self-reflection through journalism or discussions about personal goals and values. By fostering a supportive environment, parents and educators help adolescents develop the emotional intelligence they need to navigate the complexities of adolescence and transition successfully into adulthood.

In addition, it's important to teach adolescents practical emotional regulation and coping strategies that they can carry with them into adulthood. These strategies might include mindfulness practices, such as meditation or breathing exercises, which help individuals stay grounded and present during stressful situations. Teaching adolescents how to identify their emotional triggers and develop coping mechanisms for managing stress, anxiety, or anger can empower them to handle the emotional challenges they will inevitably face as they grow older. For instance, a teenager preparing for a big exam might use deep breathing exercises or positive visualization to manage their test anxiety, skills they can continue to use throughout their academic and professional careers.

Lastly, preparing adolescents for the challenges of adulthood involves encouraging them to develop a strong sense of self and purpose. Adolescents who have a clear sense of their values, passions, and goals are more likely to approach adulthood with confidence and direction. Emotional intelligence helps young people reflect on their strengths, interests, and personal motivations, allowing them to make choices that align with their long-term aspirations. For example, a high school student who is passionate about social justice might pursue a career in law or public policy, driven by their desire to make a positive impact on society. By fostering emotional intelligence, parents and educators can help adolescents cultivate a sense of purpose that guides them through the challenges and uncertainties of adulthood.

In conclusion, emotional intelligence is a lifelong asset that continues to benefit individuals as they transition from childhood to adolescence and into adulthood. By developing skills such as emotional regulation, empathy, self-awareness, and resilience, children and adolescents are better equipped to navigate the social, academic, and personal challenges they will face throughout their lives. These skills not only enhance personal relationships and career success but also contribute to overall emotional well-being and fulfillment. Through consistent support, guidance, and opportunities for growth, parents and educators can help children and adolescents build the emotional intelligence they need to thrive in adulthood and beyond.

Conclusion

Your Role in Shaping the Future

As parents, educators, and caregivers, your role in shaping the emotional intelligence of the next generation cannot be overstated. The world your children will inherit is rapidly evolving, with ever-growing social, economic, and environmental challenges. These challenges will require not only intellectual capabilities but also a deep well of emotional intelligence (EI) to navigate with resilience, empathy, and adaptability. By focusing on fostering emotional intelligence in children, you are not only preparing them to face personal and professional challenges, but also empowering them to be compassionate, ethical, and effective leaders in tomorrow's world.

Emotional intelligence starts at home, where children first learn about emotions, social dynamics, and interpersonal relationships. The environment you create, the behaviors you model, and the interactions you encourage all contribute to how a child perceives and manages their emotions. From a young age, children begin to absorb lessons about how to respond to feelings of joy, frustration, anger, and sadness. They learn how to communicate their needs, empathize with others, and regulate their emotions based on the examples set by the adults around them.

As caregivers, you play a central role in teaching emotional literacy, or the ability to recognize and understand emotions. Children often struggle to label and express their emotions because they lack the vocabulary and experience to do so. By guiding them through emotional situations—whether it's anger over a sibling rivalry or disappointment after a difficult day at school—you can teach them how to identify their feelings and articulate their needs. For instance, if your child feels frustrated after not being able to complete a puzzle, you can help them name that frustration, explaining, "It sounds like you're feeling frustrated because the puzzle was harder than you expected. Let's take a break and come back to it later." By modeling this language, you give your child the tools to manage similar emotions in the future.

In addition to emotional literacy, modeling emotional regulation is equally important. Children are constantly watching how you manage your own emotions. They learn from observing how you react when you're stressed, angry, or excited. If you handle conflict with patience and calm, they are more likely to develop those same strategies. For example, if you face a stressful situation—such as running late for an appointment—you might say aloud, "I'm feeling a bit anxious because we're running late, but let's take a deep breath and focus on getting there safely." This verbalized strategy not only helps you manage your emotions but also teaches your child a valuable emotional regulation technique they can use in their own life.

Encouraging empathy is another vital part of raising emotionally intelligent children. In a world that is becoming increasingly interconnected yet often divided, empathy will be a crucial skill for the next generation. Empathy allows children to step into someone else's shoes, understand their feelings, and respond with kindness and compassion. From a young age, children can be taught to recognize emotions in others and consider how their actions affect those around them. For example, if your child notices that a classmate is upset because they weren't included in a game, you can ask, "How do you think your friend feels right now? What could you do to help them feel better?" These conversations help children practice empathy in real-life situations, reinforcing their ability to build meaningful, supportive relationships.

Emotional intelligence is also closely tied to resilience, the ability to bounce back from adversity. Life is filled with challenges, and children need to learn how to navigate setbacks without becoming overwhelmed. As a caregiver, you can help children build resilience by teaching them how to cope with disappointment, failure, and frustration. Rather than shielding them from every difficulty, encourage them to face challenges with a growth mindset. For example, if your child fails a test, instead of focusing solely on the result, you can help them reflect on what they can learn from the experience: "I know you're upset about the test, but let's look at where you went wrong and see how you can improve for next time." By helping children view setbacks as learning opportunities, you empower them to persevere in the face of challenges.

Another important element of fostering emotional intelligence is teaching problem-solving skills. Children who are emotionally intelligent are better equipped to approach problems with a calm and constructive mindset. When a child is faced with a conflict—whether it's a disagreement with a sibling or a challenge at school—parents can guide them through the process of identifying the issue, considering different solutions, and taking action. For instance, if siblings are arguing over a toy, you might intervene by helping them express their feelings and brainstorm solutions, such as taking turns or finding a way to share. By teaching children to approach problems with patience and creativity, you help them build emotional intelligence that will serve them well throughout life.

In addition to these direct strategies, it's important to create a safe and supportive environment where children feel comfortable expressing their emotions. Emotional intelligence thrives in environments where children feel heard, respected, and valued. When children know that their feelings are valid and that they can express themselves without fear of judgment, they are more likely to develop healthy emotional habits. This doesn't mean that all emotions should be indulged without limits—boundaries are important—but it does mean that children should be encouraged to talk about how they feel and be supported in learning how to manage those emotions constructively.

In today's digital age, another important aspect of fostering emotional intelligence involves teaching children to manage emotions in the context of technology and social media. Many children and adolescents spend significant amounts of time interacting with others online, where emotional cues such as facial expressions and tone of voice are often absent. This can lead to misunderstandings, social comparison, and negative emotional experiences. As caregivers, you can help children navigate the emotional landscape of the digital world by setting healthy boundaries for screen time, encouraging face-to-face interactions, and teaching them how to respond thoughtfully to online conflicts or pressures. For example, if your child feels upset about something they saw on social media, you can help them process their emotions and reflect on how to respond, or if it's best to disengage altogether.

The long-term impact of emotional intelligence extends far beyond childhood. By helping your child develop emotional skills, you are preparing them to succeed in all areas of life—from their relationships and career to their overall mental health. Emotionally intelligent children grow into adults who are better equipped to handle stress, communicate effectively, resolve conflicts, and build meaningful connections with others. They are more likely to be resilient, adaptable, and confident in their ability to navigate life's challenges. These qualities are not only beneficial for personal success but also essential for contributing to a more empathetic and compassionate society.

As parents and educators, your role in shaping the future is both profound and far-reaching. By nurturing emotional intelligence in children, you are helping to create a generation of leaders who are not only intellectually capable but also emotionally aware. These future leaders will be better equipped to address global challenges with empathy, creativity, and collaboration. Whether they become business leaders, healthcare professionals, educators, or community organizers, emotionally intelligent individuals are more likely to lead with compassion and understanding, paving the way for a more just and equitable world.

Final Thoughts and Encouragement

Raising emotionally intelligent children is one of the most important investments you can make in their future. While academic success and cognitive skills are often prioritized, emotional intelligence is equally, if not more, critical to leading a fulfilling and successful life. Emotional intelligence helps children navigate the complexities of human relationships, manage stress, and approach challenges with resilience. It fosters empathy, self-awareness, and effective communication—skills that are essential not only for personal well-being but also for contributing to the broader community.

As you continue on this journey of raising and educating emotionally intelligent children, it's important to remember that emotional intelligence is a skill that develops over time. It's not something that can be taught in a single lesson or mastered overnight. Rather, it's a continuous process that involves patience, practice, and intentional effort. There will be moments when your child struggles to manage their emotions or navigate social situations, and that's okay. These are the moments when emotional growth happens— when your child learns, with your guidance, how to regulate their emotions, understand the feelings of others, and approach problems with a positive mindset.

Encourage your child to take ownership of their emotions, celebrate their emotional progress, and provide them with the support they need to keep growing. Remember that emotional intelligence is not about being happy all the time or avoiding negative emotions. It's about understanding, managing, and learning from all emotions—both positive and negative. By fostering emotional intelligence, you are helping your child build the emotional resilience and self-awareness they need to thrive in every aspect of their life.

In the end, raising emotionally intelligent children is not just about preparing them for personal success; it's about helping them contribute to a more compassionate, empathetic, and emotionally aware world. By investing in their emotional growth today, you are helping shape a better tomorrow for all of us.

www.ingramcontent.com/pod-product-compliance
Lightning Source LLC
Chambersburg PA
CBHW072252260726
48657CB00004BA/1299